TWO BIBLICAL FAITHS:
PROTESTANT AND CATHOLIC

TWO BIBLICAL FAITHS: PROTESTANT AND CATHOLIC

by
FRANZ J. LEENHARDT

Translated by
HAROLD KNIGHT

THE WESTMINSTER PRESS
PHILADELPHIA

PUBLISHED BY THE WESTMINSTER PRESS ®

PHILADELPHIA, PENNSYLVANIA

PRINTED IN THE UNITED STATES OF AMERICA

CONTENTS

v

AUTHOR'S FOREWORD

THE readers for whom I intend these pages are essentially the believing congregations of the churches, protestant and catholic, who are anxious to know to what extent the present divisions of the church of Christ are justified.

Some are sorry to see the reservations, the objections, the warnings, which are being multiplied on the way of advance towards unity, while they feel at times that, with the greatest warmth and sincerity, they already experience this unity. Others suffer because their aspiration towards unity is regarded as unbalanced feeling or confusion of ideas.

I would like to give both groups reasons for believing that they are not wrong to allow their faith, hope, and love to exceed the bounds, still too narrow, within which ecclesiastical wisdom from motives of prudence feels itself obliged to manoeuvre in its response to the appeals of the Holy Spirit.

It is for these that I have written, in a simple style, without any apparatus of erudition, in the hope that I may give food for their thought and prayer, in order secretly to prepare a still far-off and unforeseeable harvest.

The year in which this book was published gives it, nevertheless, in spite of myself, a certain special significance. The council convened at Rome by Pope John XXIII has an ecumenical aim. No one knows exactly how this great debate within the Roman church will develop, nor what will be its result for the non-Roman churches. Will the ecumenical intention announced at the outset have any positive results, and to what an extent and in what form?

However this may be, the high authorities who will assume responsibility for decisions may themselves also be considered as simple believers of their own church. If, on the one hand, the eminent dignity of their rank discourages any attempt to reach them, if the extent of their knowledge makes insolent any claim to instruct them, the humility of their faith on the other hand will doubtless remain disposed to examine all things, according to the exhortation of the Apostle, in order to retain what is good. It is for them too that I write.

F. L.

PREFACE

"THERE ARE THREE WORKS," said H.M. the king of Prussia, "the refutation of which I am ready to recompense with proper reward; the first is the *Symbolik* of Moehler."

Thus opens the foreword with which the French translator of Moehler's work introduced his French edition of the *Symbolik*.[1]

Whether the pages which follow are a good refutation of Moehler's *Symbolik*, H.M. the king of Prussia can no longer judge. It is certainly true, however, that in their author's intention they form a kind of refutation; but a refutation which is a way of breaking off the combat by declaring that it is wrongly engaged, and is as unworthy of the combatants as of the stakes for which it is fought.

Moehler's *Symbolik* claims to be "an exposition of the dogmatic contrarieties between catholics and protestants, according to their public confessions of faith". It has every appearance of being an objective confrontation of the two bodies. Texts are quoted.

In reality, it would be difficult to find a work which is secretly more partial. I admit that the author did not realize this. Partial none the less, his work is so for a very simple and profound reason which affects the very essence of the subject treated. Protestantism is interpreted and expounded as the development of a false idea, namely, the way in which Luther understood the primitive state of man. Stemming from this false idea, protestantism can no longer avoid the grotesque consequences of the system of thought. Catholicism, on the other hand, is understood as developing from the incarnation; the God-Man always dwells in the midst of us full of grace and truth. Hidden under human forms, the Saviour continues to act in His church.

Does the reader note the difference? Moehler understood

[1] J. A. Moehler, *La Symbolique*, trans. F. Lachat, Brussels, 1838, p. 3.

catholicism in the light of his own personal faith; he placed himself at the point of view of a believer who lives catholicism from within. He understood protestantism, on the contrary, in the light of an abstract idea, a dry and lifeless doctrine, a series of deductions; he remained alien to the basic intuition which animates protestantism; he placed himself outside the inner movement which fosters and sustains it.

No doubt H.M. the king of Prussia expected a refutation of Moehler's *Symbolik* which used the same technique and presented protestantism from within, in the light of its own essential inspiration, and catholicism from without, as an aberration of the mind.

Hence in the little work which is here offered there will be no question of the kind of refutation which His Majesty was expecting; and from the start its author resigns any claim to the promised reward. But he hopes for something better than such a reward. He would like to deserve the approbation of those who consider that the examination of other people's religious convictions can be made only on this condition: that we pierce to the heart of such convictions so as not only to perceive them with our understanding in the perspective which is proper to them, but also to associate ourselves with the rhythm of their secret pulsations and to feel something of their vital warmth.

That such a task is difficult is evident. That it is unrewarding is no less certain, for he who attempts it risks both failure and blame. We shall do our best to avoid failure. To avoid blame is more difficult. Emotions are so sensitive in all that appertains to confessional positions that it is really improbable that the sole concern for truth will be sufficient to dispel partisan hostilities.

The author entrusts himself to his readers' fair-mindedness and calm judgment. He has deemed the task too urgent to delay it in the hope of finding more favourable circumstances. Like all those who are at all familiar with ecumenical problems, he is struck by the difficulty which is experienced even by the best minds when they try to understand, "from within", the confession to which they do not personally belong. If we are protestants we always feel somewhat pained when we see a point of protestant theology expounded by a catholic, and the latter suffers no less when he reads what protestant authors say about the catholic faith. How can one help being moved on reading—and this is only one example in a hundred—what was written recently by a catholic historian who noted the utter lack of understanding shown by the protestant author of the work he was analysing with regard to the authentic catholic idea of baptism and confirmation? The homage rendered to the fairness of the author in question was so much the more moving because his fairness produced no positive result. The tragedy in fact is just this—that we must "recognize at the same time that the author seems indeed to have procured first-hand information, and shows no sign which would lead one to suspect in him a prejudiced hostility. Such an example makes us keenly aware of one of the basic difficulties of ecumenical dialogue; in spite of our using the same words, it often happens that we no longer speak the same language as our separated brethren".[1]

It is a fact. We no longer speak the same language. But what does this observation imply? What is a language? Doubtless it consists of words; but words have meaning only in virtue of the general context in which they are used, and not merely an intellectual, conceptual context, but an emotional context, the vibration of soul conferred on a language by the echo it carries within it of a whole world of experience, conscientious struggles, profound aspirations, and fundamental intuitions. Cut off from this vital soil, words are delivered up to the chances of fortuitous encounters, fallacious explanations, to the risks of distorting associations or of withering isolation.

The plan of the pages which follow is quite simply an attempt to show, in protestantism and catholicism, the historical culmination of two fundamental truths which constitute the essence of Biblical revelation. The more successful the attempt, the better will it show to the reader the living context, the theological universe, in which the "other man" lives, and will bring out the inner logic to which his thought and religious sensibility, his spirituality,

---

[1] L. Renwart, S.J., *Nouvelle Revue Théologique*, Feb. 1962, p. 214, in connection with the work of R. Voeltzel, *Education et révélation*, 1960.

and his doctrine, conform. In short, if it succeeds, it will have provided a cipher-stencil which will enable the reader to decipher the "other" in his living context, thus making it possible for him to be understood from his own point of view.

But then a further question must be asked, to which no one can today give a reply, but which it would be cowardly not to face. If the basic truths which constitute the essence of catholicism and the essence of protestantism are equally justified by Biblical revelation there emerges the problem of the relation between these two confessions which are by tradition distinct and in practice antagonistic.

TWO BIBLICAL FAITHS:
PROTESTANT AND CATHOLIC

Chapter 1

THE PROBLEM

THE reflections which will be the object of the following pages might well have deserved to be set down at greater length. In fact, a large book would hardly suffice to indicate all their possible implications. Yet we had to resign the too ambitious project of giving our subject, in the first instance, the full development to which it is entitled. Touching, as it does, on very diverse aspects of theological discipline, our theme would demand an almost universal competence in an author claiming to treat it in all its presuppositions and consequences. Biblical exegesis, church history, historical theology, dogmatics, and philosophical thought are all concerned in it in their various ways. An immense field of study would have to be mastered. Neither my culture nor the time at my disposal permit me to envisage an undertaking of this sort.

Hence, more modestly, it is a question of a simple sketch; but this sketch itself, even as reduced to very restricted dimensions in comparison with the total subject, will suffice to show that we are confronted here by a matter of primary importance. I hope that the reader will be led to a perspective from which he will be able to discern the features of a new theological landscape. The guide will consider his task completed when he has indicated the essential structure of this landscape. If he fulfils his mission suitably he will, perhaps, arouse in some the desire to go down into the plain, in order to explore in greater detail the various sectors of the complex panorama whose general outlines will have been drawn.

A universal theological competence would be needed to follow out our theme in all its consequences; but there would also be needed (and this is far more difficult of attainment) a radical purification of those habits of thinking and feeling which we owe to our environment and our education. Each one of us bears within himself a personal coefficient of understanding and—lack of understanding. The guide discloses a landscape, but he himself sees it according to his own vision and speaks of it in terms of what he has himself seen. Faced by a theological landscape, we are always more or less either myopic or colour blind. Our cultural formation has deformed us, because in training our sensibility to suffer certain reactions it has made us less apt to experience other reactions. We are both formed and deformed by the confessional situation in which we are placed; we are accustomed to certain perceptions but rebellious to others.

Non omnia possumus omnes. We are constantly tempted to reduce to our field of vision and our personal knowledge a reality from which we amputate whatever exceeds our grasp. Interconfessional dialogue furnishes at every moment the proof of a blindness with which each reproaches the other party at the very moment when he exposes himself to the same reproach. That is why wisdom counsels that we should not claim to say all. Truth is better served if we confine ourselves to affirming with prudence, leaving to others the care of completing an affirmation which could only be true because limited.

Has the dialogue between catholicism and protestantism reached an impasse?

Both the number and quality of those engaged in the discussion might lead one to believe that it is proceeding on the right lines. There is no lack of good will among those who are devoting themselves to these interconfessional exchanges. And yet one might wonder whether any progress is being made. Basic questions which constantly re-emerge remain unanswered. Certainly numerous misunderstandings are dispelled, and that is something. The real problems gradually come to light out of the muddy confusions of polemics. They are brought into better focus. But in proportion as issues become clearer, they also become more rigid. The ground which, for the sake of peace, can be yielded to one's opponent grows progressively narrower until one is driven back into a last stronghold which must be held if all is not to be lost. We cannot, on the pretext of understanding others better, cease at last to understand ourselves. Now in theological confrontation it is the whole of man's being that is engaged; it is the whole life of the believer which is at stake. In the last resort it is a question of ourselves and of our all. As interconfessional discussion progresses, it becomes ever clearer why it cannot reach a successful conclusion.

The fact is that this confrontation of catholicism and protestantism is not an intellectual or aesthetic exercise. People have too often behaved as though the dialogue was meant to bring together certain theological propositions, more or less different or opposed, and as though it was a question of comparing them by measuring the extent of the divergences between them. Now, catholicism and protestantism are less systems than men. A truth enunciated by a catholic mouth has no longer its original significance when it is heard by a protestant ear. What a protestant says to a catholic has not for the latter the same intellectual, affective, and vital resonance. Catholicism and protestantism shape the whole outlook of their adherents; they provide a language, a sensibility, a scale of values, and, one might go so far as to say, a system of logic, since it is true that the requirements of reason are to a certain extent unconsciously subordinated to the imperatives of existence and the aspirations of the heart. Man lives the truth as much as he thinks it and often much more so. Each man is led to mould the truth for himself because he lives his own life. How difficult it is for him to recognize as of vital importance a truth which is not an integral part of his own existence!

Looked at from this point of view, interconfessional discussions do not always seem to have reached a depth appropriate to their goal. Man is not a catholic or protestant because he adopts such or such a theological concept, such or such a dogma. What makes the protestant is not the fact that he quotes the Bible, any more than what makes a catholic is the fact that he quotes Denzinger. Protestants and catholics are what they are, fundamentally, because they cherish a certain inner attitude, because they have adopted a certain basic position which affects their whole being and increasingly determines all their intellectual and emotional reactions. Dogmatic propositions strike both alike as true just in so far as they are congruous with this basic position, this life of the soul whose characteristic exigences colour all their judgments. Faith is an experience which lives by its object before becoming a doctrinal elaboration of that experience. God reveals Himself to a soul before the believer begins to speak of the revelation. It is from this ineffable revelation, from the way in which it impinges on the soul at the very centre of its life, that all the intellectual and emotional reactions then flow which will crystallize and clarify it. In this sense, doctrines and dogmas are secondary, and a confrontation at the level of such remains perforce alien to the heart of the matter. It is necessary to penetrate to the fundamental intuition which is their inspiring source and which justifies them in their place.

It has been said that catholics and protestants have not the same God—a remark which at first sight will appear scandalous and quite contrary to the ecumenical spirit. It is a remark, however, in which we shall see some truth, if we are prepared to see in it an allusion to that basic intuition which governs the structure of the whole *theo*-logy of our two confessions. Have catholics and protestants, at their point of departure, the same intuitive understanding of God? Does God's self-revelation strike them in the same way? Do they apprehend the mystery of the divine according to the same criteria? To these questions we must give a negative reply and understand that here precisely lies the decisive point.

Interconfessional confrontation becomes entangled in problems without real importance, if it does not strike sufficiently deep to reach this initial and determinative antithesis. Problems raised will remain unsolved so long as effects only are considered without any concern to penetrate to their underlying causes.

Perhaps it will be said in reply that catholicism and protestantism have in common Holy Scripture, which ought to be sufficient to solve their problems. Both confessions recognize its authority. Hence it is on the ground of scriptural exegesis that the debate should be carried on. The hope might be entertained that here at least, at the cost of patient and honest labour, antagonisms could be appeased. The common God of Christians is the God of Abraham, Isaac, and Jacob, the God of Jesus Christ. Why decree irreducible conflicts between them when both draw from the same source of revelation the same knowledge of the same God?

Who would not wish to see this thought embodied in facts? In principle, scripture unites us, protestants with catholics, catholics with protestants. In fact, our two confessions read Holy Scripture in two different ways. In spite of our common desire to listen to the Word of God, we do not hear the same message!

It is true that professional exegetes are now often reconciled on many points which formerly were the object of severe controversy. Their better understanding is certainly an encouraging sign. But it is a far cry from the analytic explanation of texts, which is the special task of the exegete, to the doctrinal constructions which the churches inevitably add to them. From the same stones very different edifices can be built. Now scripture does not furnish the architectural plan of the doctrinal cathedral which shelters a particular communion. The confessions have been obliged to run the risks of dogmatic adventure. It is here that difficulties arise and even increase, since each party holds that its particular construction is the only one authorized by scripture and accuses his opponent of not being faithful to their common criterion. The dispute becomes acrimonious. When brothers become enemies they are more bitter in their antagonisms, since they betray that brotherhood which unites them in spite of everything.

Interconfessional confrontation must penetrate to this initial opposition which lies at the very source of all authority. It is true that scripture unites us, protestants and catholics; but it is no less true that it is scripture also which divides us. Each believer finds in it the ultimate reason for not yielding to the contrary point of view. It divides us the more seriously in that both parties sincerely hope to remain faithful to it. It would be too easy a solution in this matter to be content with suspecting the good faith of one's interlocutor. We must indeed concede to our opponents that

17

measure of good will and sincerity which we ask them to be so good as to recognize in us from the outset. But why, then, do we not agree on a single explanation of scripture which would remove our disagreement at its source?

Of course, the solution of the problem cannot reside in the doctrine of the church's teaching authority, a doctrine which catholic theologians readily invoke when the problems which now concern us are discussed with them. Their argument is roughly as follows: protestantism has no right to claim to put forward an interpretation of scripture which conflicts with that which catholicism considers to be the true one, for the Roman church alone has received from Jesus the true knowledge of His thought, together with the power of expounding it and the duty of teaching it. In this matter protestantism is foreclosed. On principle, there is only one interpretation of scripture possible, which is that contained in the church's authoritative teaching.

This argument could only convince those who are already convinced, for it turns in a vicious circle. One might ask indeed in what name the teaching authority of the church asserts that it is invested with the power of expounding scripture infallibly, inerrantly. The reply cannot be in doubt, and there is only one possible reply, that which has just been suggested: the church authority has received this power from Jesus Christ, the church's founder, as is said in the 16th chapter of the Gospel according to St. Matthew in the very famous declaration of the Lord to the apostle Peter. Now does this declaration, the importance of which no one disputes, say explicitly what it is made to say? Something must be added to the text to find in it the meaning which the Roman church lends to it.

Thus appears the circle in which the argument is enclosed: it is claimed that the church's teaching authority is justified by the text, but it is that very authority which imposes its interpretation on the text which ought to justify it. In itself alone, left to its own sole evidence, Christ's word to Peter does not justify the authority claimed by the church, yet it is on that word that everything rests.

It is not that the good faith of catholic exegetes is the issue here, it is rather that the insoluble character of the whole discussion reveals the difficulty against which every inter-confessional encounter stumbles. Let us repeat that catholics and protestants read the same texts in all good faith, but do not find them to yield the same teaching.

Why is it thus? The question must not be asked in regard to any particular text. The problem is not that of knowing why catholic and protestant interpretations of certain basic texts diverge or even clash. No one text, however important, is self-sufficient. A scriptural text is always included in the wider scope of a more general reading; it is part of the total movement of Biblical thought.

If the two confessions ascribe to such or such texts varying degrees of importance and draw from them divergent con-clusions, the ultimate reason is that each confession gives to its interpretation of scripture as a whole an orientation which is not in harmony with the approach made by the opposite party. It is not merely a question of discussion about detail: the divergence has to do with the interpretation of scripture as a whole. This makes the matter so much the more serious! Protestants and catholics, we do not read Holy Scripture in the same way. Is it possible, then, to read scripture in two different ways?

For many years now, I have frequented quite perseveringly the circles in which both catholic and protestant exegesis was taught; I have tried to understand with as much ob-jectivity as possible the dogmatic constructions built upon the conclusions yielded by exegesis and developed according to what the one and the other party deemed to be the potenti-ality of Biblical teaching. I have found it impossible always to justify one confessional perspective as opposed to the other. I have been convinced that many truths disputed by one of the antagonists rested upon bases as solid as the truths with which they conflicted. Each for his part and from his own point of view finds solid support in the texts on which he concentrates his attention. Again and again it has seemed to me that the exegetical deductions of the two parties, in-stead of clashing, proceeded on parallel lines, starting from premises that were different but equally Biblical, premises that were, however, unfortunately limited and hence partial. Each one was right, but from his own point of view. The common mistake was not to keep sight of all the texts, with the result that each warped the conclusions he drew and ended with generalizations that were improper or even downright erroneous. It seems to me that the good faith of each party comes to grief by reason of the very complexity of scripture to which no one does full justice in spite of the sincerest wish of his heart. There are more things in the Word of God than our confessional theologies know how to—or find it possible to—retain.

Facts speak very clearly in the same sense. The current and traditional education of the protestant furnishes him with at least elementary ideas about the Letters to the Romans and Galatians, but he feels himself somewhat lost when he reads the Letters to the Ephesians or the Colossians, to say nothing of certain passages of the First Letter to the Corinthians. The dogmatic teaching of protestantism draws amply upon the rich stores of the Letters to the Romans and the Galatians, and it is the theme of justification by faith which lies at their heart. There is no reason to regret that this fundamental truth is given a place of honour; but one must recognize that the emphasis on this doctrine has become so exclusive that the protestant hardly knows in consequence how to deal with the teachings relative to the church developed in the Letters to the Ephesians and Colossians. To be sure, I can well understand that the catechism in current use in certain Roman Catholic dioceses does not even mention the doctrine of justification by faith. For catholicism, the teaching authority of the church decides how scripture must be read; if it amputates scripture, it shows its authority, confesses its choice, and assumes its responsibilities. But I can understand less easily why protestantism has so often been reluctant frankly to assimilate certain aspects of Biblical teaching.

Whether deliberately or not, catholics and protestants always return to the same texts, but the texts adopted by either side are different. Each takes a certain set of truths as supplying the key to scripture and reads scripture in a unilateral way. He can hardly conceive that it might be possible to proceed on different lines, for his whole education and the whole tradition of his own church fetters him to that particular perspective. History weighs heavily on the interpretation of the Bible, not only through the inertia of formed habits, but through the pressure which these exercise on judgment.[1]

The history of the Christian church of the west has canalized the reading of scripture along two main currents of approach.

This is not the place to sketch a picture of the state of Roman Catholicism in the 16th century when Luther raised the protest which was to unleash a vast reforming movement in the church. An institution centuries old preserved a dazzling heritage, but found itself implicated in burdensome compromises with the world, especially as regards those things which constitute the world's greatest misery, money and misconduct. Its spirituality had become weakened and distorted; superstition and legalism had often taken place of religious fervour and true obedience. A type of thought which was over-subtle, verging on sophistry, obscured the glow of those truths which fire the soul of the believer. Catholic historians today admit that the revolt of Luther was largely justified in view of the state of the church at the time. They discriminate between the sanctity of the church and the wretchedness of the men who at that time served it. They do not reproach Luther with having denounced the faults of men but with not having respected the holiness of the church. It is not what he attempted to do but the way in which he did it which led him into the ways of heresy and schism; he lifted his hand against his mother.

Let us not try to settle the delicate question of the rights and duties of the prophetic office in the church. The fact is that Luther's revolt presented itself as a vindication of the need for remaking and restoration addressed to an institution which the weight of centuries had humanized and secularized to an excessive degree. The aspirations of the Christian soul, athirst for renewal, could the more easily be realized in

[1] See, in this connection, F. Leenhardt, "Sola Scriptura ou Ecriture et Tradition", *Etudes théologiques et religieuses*, Montpellier, 1961.

consequence of that flow of ideas which impelled humanism to return to the sources. A desire was generally felt to experience a direct contact with the gospel in all its pristine freshness. Faith joyfully discovered the power of the word which God addresses to each individual soul through the testimony of the scriptures. In such a return to sources there was no touch of the archeologist's coquetry, but rather the contagious exultation of those who have once tasted the thirst-quenching, life-giving spring. One must not any more assign the principal role to the political circumstances of the hour or the personal temperament of Luther. That would be a convenient way of dispensing with the need to recognize the true responsibilities and the true issues at stake in the matter. It was the Christian conscience which protested once more against a sick institution and those who had corrupted it. Unfortunately the servants of the church confounded their own persons with the church which they served. But the protests of the awakened Christian conscience nevertheless jostled the very justice of men. The gospel of grace made a triumphant penetration into the church.

To be sure, the church had not erased this gospel from the corpus of its dogmas. But what had it done to ensure that the vivifying essence of dogma was transmitted from the canonical documents to the piety of the faithful? The Christian God of the time was terrible and far-off, demanding many a penance for the gift of a parsimoniously hoarded grace harshly administered by an unenlightened clergy. Men exhausted themselves in the performance of meritorious acts. They lived in a state of anxious piety, the rigours of which did not suffice to calm the scruples it fostered. Luther had known this deep dissatisfaction. He realized one day at last that the gospel is a piece of good news, really good, and, in comparison with all that man has a right to expect, really news. The God of Jesus Christ was revealed to him as the God of free grace, the God who had turned in His compassion to the poor and humble. Instead of a God who was inert and accountable, Luther discovered a God who was active and generous, whose graces were forestalling and decisive.

It was through the Letters to the Galatians and Romans that God revealed Himself to Luther in this new light. Justification by faith and by faith alone without the concurrence of works, a response to God's promise which is seized by faith in the One who will perform it and that apart from the weight of meritorious works, such was the gospel which Luther read into the writings of the apostle to the Gentiles.

One cannot fail to note the position occupied, in those two letters on which Luther principally drew, by the figure of Abraham, the very type of the believer to whom Paul recurs with significant emphasis. Certainly, Jewish tradition had not failed to throw into prominence the figure of the patriarch; but it chose to insist on the merit which Abraham had acquired by bearing his only son to the altar of sacrifice. Paul is not at all interested in the episode to which the rabbis attached supreme importance. It is not what man has done but what God does which attracts his attention. Paul emphasizes God's promise, the word intervening from On High, the word which creates a wholly new situation, and accomplishes God's purpose apart from man's collaboration. Abraham's faith and obedience do not participate in this accomplishment; they constitute the response which is fitting to a divine promise, that is to say, the confidence that He who has made the promise will ensure its fulfilment.

The accession of St. Paul and with him of Abraham to the forefront of the theological scene stood in strong contrast to the importance which the church had traditionally attributed to St. Peter. The details of the process which gradually culminated in the ordinance that the bishop of Rome was the accredited successor of the apostle Peter, matter little. The central fact is that the *Tu es Petrus* had become the cornerstone of the Roman edifice. It was destined to impose itself as of decisive importance, to the extent of forming, as it were, a gold-lettered crown encircling the head of Peter's vicar enthroned beneath the immense cupola of the church dedicated to the prince of the apostles; and over the head of the sovereign pontiff the cupola with its inscription represented a formidable tiara.

It is legitimate to suggest that the conflict which arose

when the protestants demanded a reform of the church is an echo of the conflict which, in the church's earliest days, brought into opposition the apostles Peter and Paul. Without exaggerating, it may be asserted that the chief concern of Paul was to free the Christian faith from the fetters of the Mosaic law, whereas Peter was tempted to "judaize"; this expression from the pen of Paul is the essential reproach which he addresses to Peter (Gal. 2:14). Paul intended to react against the Mosaic influence which Peter still wished to maintain at the heart of the Christian community.

Thus, behind Paul may be seen looming the great personality of Abraham. Behind Peter there arises likewise a personality of capital importance, namely, Moses.

We must be careful to note that the clash between Peter and Paul did not terminate in a complete rupture. The distrust of the apostle to the Gentiles, or even his hostility to the tendencies that were fostered by preference in Jerusalemite circles, never led this man "born out of due time" (1 Cor. 15:8) to disown his solidarity with the mother-church of Jerusalem. Paul never forgot that Moses was an integral part of the divine revelation and had prophesied the coming of the Messiah. He refers to Moses at every opportunity. It was in the books of Moses that he sought and found those categories of thought which enabled him to interpret the scandal of the cross. The law of Moses was in his eyes interwoven into the economy of salvation; he attacked an erroneous and improper interpretation of the law, but not the law itself, which he restored to its essential place in the whole structure of the promises.

Thus the church of Jesus Christ was placed beneath the exclusive sign neither of Abraham nor of Moses. The Petrine influence did not efface the Pauline. We know little of the discussions which took place at that time, but we do know enough to realize that the church preserved its organic and doctrinal unity, despite the seeds of division latent in such profoundly different orientations.

In this connection let us observe that protestant historians and theologians are placed in a situation which is both advantageous and perilous. On the one hand, through the extant letters we are in some measure informed about the person and the doctrines of the apostle Paul. On the other hand, the figures of Peter and James, the patrons and ancestors of Roman Catholicism, are glimpsed only in blurred outline through our documents. The result is that the presentation which the New Testament gives of the historical and theological reality of the first church runs a grave risk of being distorted and unilateral. Protestants are tempted to believe that the origins of the church were entirely dominated by the personality and the thought of Paul. They are inclined to reduce primitive Christianity to Paulinism. Catholics are better able to resist this tendency, because their previous dogmatic training, entirely governed by the figure of Peter and controlled by preoccupations relative to church organization, makes them more perceptive of indications left in the texts by the current of thought proceeding from the apostle Peter. A sense of proportion should warn protestant exegetes and theologians not to abuse a situation which is, after all, contingent.

It is not our task now to follow, in the further development of the history of the church, the influence which each of the two great "patrons" of primitive Christianity was destined to exert. Rather our interest must be centred less on them than on the two patriarchal figures which foreshadow and explain them, Abraham and Moses. Protestantism through Paul refers us back to Abraham, and catholicism through Peter to Moses: in the last analysis, it is to these initiating heroes that we must go back in order to try to find in them the underlying reasons for those characteristics which differentiate the two divergent traditions that, it might be claimed, emanate from them.

Chapter 2

THE SPIRITUALITY OF ABRAHAM CONTRASTED
WITH THE SPIRITUALITY OF MOSES

ABRAHAM and Moses; the two figures who stand to the
fore of Biblical revelation.

Abraham, the man struck by an unexpected word;
the man torn from all that he has been and cast into a totally
new destiny by a stupendous call. Nothing prepares him
for the event which happens to him. Everything comes to
him from outside, from some sphere where he is not and of
which he knows nothing. Further emphasizing the home-
lessness which is thus imposed on him, the voice of God involves him in an unforeseeable adventure; he will have
to leave his country, his familiar surroundings, his family,
his religious and mental habits, deny himself as regards all
that constituted his existence and personality, in order that
he may go to meet a totally unknown future. His vocation
cannot rest on any element in his past, nor on any prevision
of his future. It obliges him to count only on what God has
said to him, on God's word, God's promise. He will have to
receive day by day, and each day afresh, that which is to
constitute his present. He will have to live in the moment,
that is to say in faith, in utter dependence, in an obedient
attention to God's promise, which is his sole security, his
sole ground for exceeding the present moment by the power
of hope.

Thus Abraham becomes the archetypal believer, the man
of faith, the man divested of any support because he demands no other security than that of God's promise; the
believer whose trust in the promise makes him at the same
time a participant in the power of the God who has spoken
and who fulfils what His word declares.

It is well known that Jewish tradition underlined the merits of Abraham by pointing to the obedience of which he had given proof in consenting to the sacrifice of Isaac. But St. Paul is not interested in what Abraham may have done; he does not even mention the meritorious gesture which was of supreme interest to Judaism. On the contrary, he emphasizes what Abraham did not do, and in particular what he could not do. For him, it is a question of insisting on the incapacity of the patriarch. If he is led to remind us of what Abraham did, it is in fact with the evident intention of stressing that he ought not to have done it. Just where Abraham imagined that he had some power, it is his powerlessness which is most vividly disclosed. This is the case in regard to the patriarch's adventure with Hagar, his maid, whence Ishmael will be the issue (Gal. 4:21-31). The emergence of Ishmael plays the part of the shadows in the picture which throw into greater relief the brilliance of its colours and define the perspective by giving depth to the vision of things. Abraham as the father of Ishmael represents the incredulity of the believer who does not trust in the promise with sufficient faith to leave its fulfilment to the sole power of the One who has made it. God declared that a posterity would spring from the centenarian couple. Abraham is convinced that Sarah cannot bear him a child. He finds a way of evading the difficulty so that Sarah's old age shall not be an obstacle to the fulfilment of the promise. He produces a child by his union with Hagar his slave. Ishmael is the off-spring of this unbeliever's act.

With Ishmael St. Paul contrasts Isaac, born of Sarah, the true son of the promise and the true gift of the God who made the promise. Isaac does not owe his birth to the flesh, he is the son according to the promise, according to the Spirit.

Why? Because Abraham and Sarah have received this son as God's gift, as the fruit of the promise in which they believed. The manner in which Paul evokes the situation of the centenarian couple is characteristic (Rom. 4:19). His emphasis on the "necrosis" ($\nu\epsilon\kappa\rho\omega\sigma\iota\varsigma$) of Abraham and Sarah is meant to bring out the fact that the expected event will owe nothing to the intervention of man, even of man as believer. The promise is accomplished by the sole power of

God's intervention. Those concerned cannot in any way co-operate.

Paul's commentary on this significant event is rendered no less significant by the way in which he defines the being of the God who fulfils His promise. The faith of Abraham is his trust in a God "who gives life to the dead and calls into existence the things that do not exist" (Rom. 4:17). The God of Abraham then is the One who brings to the service of His promise that sovereignty which is manifested in His power to create and to give life even to that which is dead.

As an exegete of the narratives relative to Abraham, St. Paul has shown a penetrating insight into the dual character of God's self-revelation to the patriarch as the God of the promise. Two features characterize Abraham's God: His creative power and His vivifying power. These two features are strictly related to the dual certitude of the believer faced by the promise, for the promise which declares what God will do signifies that the past is radically challenged and that the present only subsists through that very act which delivers it from its factualness, from the dead weight of the "already done", to transform it into a new reality which is rich with the virtualities of the future. Confronted by the God of the promise, Abraham discovers that he is not imprisoned in his creaturely past, blocked in his creaturely being, congealed in a nature which would immobilize him by putting him outside the scope of that sovereign intervention which God announces in making His promise. Abraham learns to know God as the One who constantly sustains His creatures by His creative power. God is revealed to him as the One who has not abandoned His creation to a fate determined once for all, to a history overshadowed by some destiny, providential but immutable. The God of Abraham's faith is not the motionless first mover, nor the watchmaker constructing his watch. He is the God present in the very act of creation. And thence flows likewise the fact that Abraham's God takes in charge even man's present after having taken in charge his past. He stands self-revealed to the patriarch as the God who makes the dead to live. The image is as powerful as possible. Man confronted by the God of the promise cannot but discover his state of powerlessness, his radical "necrosis" and "weakness"; in the face of God he cannot but confess that, although alive according to the flesh, he is dead as far as the object of the promise is concerned, dead according to the spirit. God reveals Himself to Abraham as the God who comes forward to vivify this present, to transform it by endowing it with virtualities which it did not possess, to cast into this barren soil a seed which will one day blossom.

It may be useful to dwell on this second aspect of God's self-revelation to Abraham by referring to an observation made in the Letter to the Hebrews. The author compares to a resurrection the fact that Abraham received back his son after having placed him on the altar of Moriah (Hb. 11:17-19). The promise always runs the risk of being understood as something acquired, as a possession granted, as capital amassed, which the beneficiary may dispose of as he pleases. Faith is always threatened by the temptation to take the divine move as a mode in which God alienates His own liberty. It must ceaselessly be reminded that God not only gives life in the beginning, but gives it at every moment anew; that God not only pronounces the promise in sovereign freedom, but does not cease freely to make and renew the promise at every instant as though it had never been made. Faith must agree to recognize the liberty of God as regards whatever of His being is accessible to the believer. It is then only that faith can live out every moment of its life in God's presence as something truly and actually vouchsafed by God, at each instant anew. For want of confessing this sovereign freedom of God, faith would fetter God to His self-manifestations, and would reduce His being to the dimensions of His self-revelation, that is to say, would adapt Him to the measure of the knowledge which the feeble faith of man has been able to apprehend of Him.

It is this, then, that the author of the Letter to the Hebrews wishes to emphasize by his allusion to resurrection in connection with the sacrifice of Isaac (11:17-19). Not only does Abraham recognize that faith's submission to the promise places the latter in a position of complete dependence on divine intervention; but he recognizes further that the obedience of faith makes the believer at every moment of his existence totally dependent on the promise and on the divine action which realizes it. Isaac was, however, God's gift, God's workmanship, the sign of His grace, the very substance of the promise; in consequence, a good which faith ought to have been able to consider as solidly gained, a gift which it might have seemed impossible that God could revoke without denying Himself, without lapsing into capricious and self-contradictory ways, since everything depended on it.

Now the revelation of the transcendent freedom of grace is so strong in the soul of the patriarch that it leads him to accept as the very will of God the sense of obligation to sacrifice his son Isaac. It has been asked whether the requirement of God in this matter was not a barbarism unworthy of the God of Jesus Christ; it has been thought that Abraham was the victim of the savage customs of the time, the episode of the sacrifice of Isaac being no more than the last vestige of a religion which still demanded human sacrifice; in this case the greatness of Abraham would consist in his power of rising above the religiosity of primitive man. To understand the matter thus is to miss the true aim and significance of the narrative. Sacrifice as a concrete act has to do only with the expression of sentiments, and this expression depends in fact on the mental habits of each individual. It is a short-sighted anachronism to object that the patriarch could not have believed that God would require such a sacrifice of him. But God in fact required him to advance in the way of faith up to that perilous and salutary point at which God counts for more than the graces He has bestowed, at which all grace, to remain gracious, can and must be called in question, without ever becoming crystallized in a past event, in order that God may ever remain sovereign over His gifts, and His grace ever present and actual. The sacrifice of Isaac means that grace does not become capital that may be exploited, does not become an inalienable assurance for Abraham's faith, but that the patriarch receives every day afresh both the promise and its realization.

This faith deprived of all assurance is ignorant of anything that might bring its object into focus. The God of Abraham reveals Himself as the One who is present only in His word, who is active in His promise alone, which He himself realizes. We shall see that Moses learns from the revelation of His God how he must name Him. There is nothing similar in the case of Abraham, and the silence is certainly significant.[1] A name gives a certain measure of security. One knows whom to address. The faith of Abraham is far too much centred on the mystery of God's freedom to agree that God should be enshrined in any word whatsoever. God leaves no trace of His presence. He reveals Himself in the vocation and the promise, in the revelatory act, but nothing prolongs the revelation on the plane of human contingencies. The God of Abraham is there when He calls, when He speaks, when He is heard, when man "lives" with Him. He is present in an actuality which would be compromised by an objectivization in the shape of the divine character and attributes. In tradition He will be designated as "the God of Abraham, of Isaac, and of Jacob", that is to say as the One who is inseparable from the living experience which the patriarchs had of Him, beyond which nothing more can be affirmed of Him, and without which nothing can be known of Him. Pascal emphasized this point by opposing this God to the God of the philosophers. In the one case a God who speaks; in the other a God about whom man speaks. Therein lies the whole difference! Here, a God whose reality is known to the heart; there, a God whose reality is objectivized in concepts.

Abraham's God reveals Himself when He wills. His intervention in the life of the patriarch depended on nothing. It was the effect of His decision alone. This God is entirely free with regard to historical contingencies, with the result that His intervention obliged Abraham to make a radical rupture with the past. Nothing permitted man to foresee either that God would speak or what He would say. Similarly, nothing permits man to foresee that God will continue the dialogue He has begun; nothing, except His own word, His engagement, His promise. Faith was not able

---

[1] On the name *El Shaddai*, see below, p. 40.

to rest for support on anything prior to the word; nor can it find support in anything following the word. It can count only on God's own faithfulness.

It is true nevertheless that the story of the patriarch does give a certain place to visible and concrete signs of the promise granted to Abraham. His faith does not shrink from asking for attestations, and it was granted him to see the smoking furnace and the flames passing between the divided pieces of the heifers. He received even the permanent sign of circumcision, to recall the covenant which God had made with him.

These facts warn us that we must not arbitrarily simplify reality. Indisputably, it is not such facts, however, which impart to the faith of Abraham its essential characteristics. We must rather agree with St. Paul and the New Testament in general, which attach no importance to them in the interpretation they give of Abraham's significance for the history of revelation. It is especially noteworthy that Paul does indeed refer to circumcision but only in order to emphasize that it comes after the promise. It is brought in to bear witness to the word of the promise. For the apostle what counts is the promise which founds the covenant, hence the initial move of God and His lasting fidelity. The covenant does not rest on circumcision; the sons of Abraham are circumcised because they have been welcomed by God into the covenant, not the converse.

As we shall see later on, this way of understanding the sign is very different from the interpretation which the sign receives in the context of Mosaic faith and spirituality; there, it will not refer back to the word as an attestation of the promise contained in the word, as a sign of God's fidelity; the Mosaic sign is to be referred rather to the "descent" of God, and must be understood as a sign of the presence of God.

None the less, it will be noted that the word of God is already accompanied by those visible and concrete signs whose function will be characteristic of the Mosaic faith. This shows that the dialectic explicitly maintained by the Abrahamic and Mosaic types of faith exists at the very heart of each of them. In the former case the sign accompanies the word, just as in the latter case the word is the foundation of the sign.

The initial grace of God remains, then, the basis of Abraham's faith. It remains also the basis of Abraham's hope. Nothing of what God gives may become a guarantee of what He will give. The believer clings to the Giver, not to the gift. Only by this attitude can his life truly turn on the axis of the promise. To have centred his attention on the gift of grace would have been to turn away from the promise and from the One who made it and wills to fulfil it. Abraham's faith never becomes self-enclosed so as to be stabilized in what it has received; it is ever open towards the horizons of the future unveiled by the promise. That is why Abraham takes to the altar of Moriah not his son only, but the gift of circumcision likewise. The gift must always remain a gift, and for that purpose faith must ever and again call it in question as a gift that has been received. Failing this questioning and surrender, the divine gift is perverted into something that man possesses, and the believer who has thus become a capitalist can for a moment dispense with the need to seek and receive all from God. For Abraham, it is only the way of perpetual oblation which can lead to plenitude. The believer advances towards his undisclosed future. Abraham, living in the strength of the promise, is not the man he has been, but the man he will be. The past of Abraham does not become for him the means and the occasion for dispensing with God. His life is wholly turned towards his future. His existence is eschatological. All is future for him, because all comes from God. Time for Abraham is the form in which he experiences the transcendence of God.

In his Letter to the Romans (chapter 4) Paul did not dwell on Abraham's adventure with Hagar. He did not, however, fail to seize its meaning. In the Letter to the Galatians He explicitly evokes the circumstance. There are two Abrahams, two attitudes, just as there are two covenants and similarly two Jerusalems (Gal. 4:21-31). There is the Abraham of Hagar and the Abraham of Sarah, just as there is the earthly Jerusalem and the heavenly Jerusalem. The Abraham who went in to Hagar is the man who lived according to the norms of given, natural existence, the man who was the slave of his past, who did not believe that his true existence lay before him as a grace to be received from his God; an unbelieving and carnal Abraham, that is to say, one who trusted in the "flesh", in his own strength, in himself. The believing Abraham is content to live eschatologically, by virtue of the promise to come, and in the expectation of its fulfilment by the One who has made it; the man liberated from what he has been and open to receive the future which God foreshadows for him. This contrast is symbolized in the antithesis between the two Jerusalems. The earthly Jerusalem objectifies the past, embodies carnal existence and bondage. The heavenly Jerusalem represents the future accessible to faith through the promise, adumbrates what the believer waits to receive and which, coming from heaven as something radically new, is contrasted with what comes from the earth, from the "world". These two cities correspond to the two wives whom Abraham knew: the one, Hagar, offers us the face of Abraham's unbelief, while Sarah pictures to us the face of faith.

Thus the vision which scripture gives us of Abraham's faith constitutes a coherent whole. The case of Abraham implies a theology, a certain revelation of God as the God oı absolute initiatives and of the grace which, itself alone, completes the work which it has begun. This theology controls a certain understanding of man: faced by the God of Abraham, man discovers his true condition, which is what Paul described as a state of "necrosis". This anthropology and this theology condition the only soteriology conceivable for the man who avows his necrosis in face of God's promise; salvation can be only the work of God, Himself accomplishing His promise.

It is the God of Abraham, of Isaac, and of Jacob who reveals Himself to Moses (Ex. 3:6). One could hardly expect from a study of the position of Moses that it would bring to light a contradiction in the development of the faith of Israel. But just because there is development we shall expect to find change and complement, and, if we consider the circumstances, it is easy to foresee in what sense the development will take place.

With Abraham, God laid the foundation of an absolute beginning. This is no longer the case with Moses, who inherits a revelation and enters into an existing situation. Abraham left all and found himself alone, in radical rupture both with his past and with himself, cruelly constrained to undergo the dual experience of the impotence of his past and his present, of the "world" and of himself. Moses belongs to a community to which he is bound by bonds he will not be required to break, but rather to utilize so as to bring the people of his race to accept the new revelation which has been granted them. The father of believers looks up to heaven, whence will spring that promised posterity, whereas the prophet of Sinai looks down at the mass of this people, who already constitute the posterity of Abraham. All is rupture and discontinuity in the life of the man who comes from Ur of the Chaldees and who is destined one day to climb the slopes of Moriah. The work of Moses is rooted in a past which it sanctions and organizes; it is already linked to a tradition. Moses comes before us as a "son of the Hebrews".

As was the case with Abraham, God's revelation to Moses takes place through a word. But with Abraham the word was within; for Moses it is inscribed without in concrete, visible circumstances, capable of affecting the senses. While He thus reveals Himself as nearer and more accessible, since He is manifested on the plane of earthly realities, the God of Moses reveals Himself as more distant, more mysterious, more terrible. At the very moment when man believes it possible to approach Him, he is gripped by the infinite grandeur of the divine.

Two scenes embody the Mosaic revelation of God, that on Mount Horeb and that on Sinai. At Horeb it is God revealing Himself in a flame which kindles a bush. God is there, on that familiar soil where He has come to seek out Moses, condescending to place Himself on a level with this shepherd, making Himself known to him as he watches his flocks. There are neither thunders nor trumpets, but a voice and a dialogue; Moses is called by his name. Presence of God, of a God who has drawn near; mysterious presence, however, although showing itself to be so near. The bush burns, but is not consumed, states the narrative of Moses' vision (Ex. 3:2). The symbol signifies a presence which both contradicts the things by which it is manifested and nevertheless takes them in charge. This presence burns; it should reduce to ashes, for God is in no way assimilable to this bush and His presence consumes it. But in fact the bush is not consumed, because God is revealing Himself. Were it consumed, the bush would not serve to *reveal* the mystery of God. Did it not burn, it would not serve to reveal the *mystery of God*. The symbol conveys what it intends to convey about the God of Moses, who is both near and mysterious, who enters into the course of this world, but without confounding Himself with this world, who burns it rather from within, so as to make it serve to reveal His mysterious presence.

On Sinai Moses takes knowledge of his God as a hidden God, a God of terrors and lightnings. Here is the God whose word is confounded with the angry roar of thunder, whose approach is manifested in storm and lightning flash, who wreathes the mountain with smoke like the smoke of a kiln. The mountain quakes because Yahweh must descend upon it (Ex. 19:18). Confronted by this spectacle, Moses recoiled and shuddered (Hb. 12:21) while the people, even more dismayed, begged to be spared and implored not to hear the terrible voice: "You speak to us and we will hear; but let not God speak to us, lest we die" (Ex. 20:19). The voice of God, which in the scene of the burning bush reveals the divine redemptive plan, here makes the Israelites tremble with fear lest they should be annihilated. And Moses, while the people stood afar off, so as to avoid supremely dangerous contacts, drew near to the "sombre darkness".[1] This translation is perhaps, certainly even, somewhat forced; but it has the advantage of evoking a well-known mystical experience, which must be recognized in the symbolic picture drawn in the Book of Exodus. Moses comes to know what mystical tradition has called the dark night of the soul, that divine nearness which abolishes the earthly experience of sunlight in order to flood the soul of the contemplative with true

[1] Fr. *La sombre ténèbre*, Ex. 20:21; translation Crampon-Bonsirven.

light. The God of fire disclosed on Sinai banishes from Moses all the "light" of this world; it is in a thick cloud that He hides. His mystery is so much the more impenetrable that He must have recourse to the heavenly fire in order to make Himself known. The symbol of lightning, the absolute light which rends the cloud which human sight cannot pierce, serves admirably to suggest the transcendence of the God who comes down to save His people.

For, let us not forget—and the point may summarize the whole revelation of which Moses is the bearer—the God of Moses is a God who descends to this earthly sphere. He brings Himself into solidarity with the men whose wretchedness He has noted, that handful of miserable slaves suffering in Egypt. The translation of the French Rabbinate for the text Ex. 3:8 makes God speaking to Moses say: "I have *intervened.* . . ." The expression is incorrect; the Hebrew *yarad* means to *descend*. This is much stronger and more explicit, and one wonders what motive, to be sure an unconscious one, caused the Jewish translators to avoid the word *descend* which already in fact evokes the characteristic theme of the incarnation.[1]

The God of Moses descends to earth. He becomes implicated in the realities of this world because He wills to save His people and in order to give them the means of revelation and salvation appropriate to the level of the human condition. He renders Himself present and manifests His presence mysteriously. He is there, without in a sense being there; the cloud veils and discloses Him at one and the same time, like the bush which is aflame when the eye of faith pierces its natural insignificance. This God can appoint a meeting with man: "Behold, there is a place by me . . ." (Ex. 33:21); but He merely passes by and man can but see His back; none can look upon His face and live (Ex. 33:20). This simple language has great reverberation and depth, such as it is hardly possible to formulate in abstract terms. It intends to convey the truth that God is very near, although He may not be localized and does not occupy space in the same way as man does who may be said to be

---

[1] They retain the word, however, in connection with the descent of God on Sinai (Ex. 19:18).

somewhere. He is present, but is not enclosed in a defined space, nor is He a prisoner of the mode of His presence. He is not to be confounded with the means by which He makes Himself present and approachable. Nevertheless, He is here. There are sacral places in which He may be encountered, and Moses indeed will be able to enter the tent to converse familiarly with Him, face to face, as a man speaks with his friend (Ex. 33:11).

Abraham was alone; Moses is faced by a people for whom God has made him responsible. It is as the God of this people that He reveals Himself to Moses. After breaking with his past Abraham was face to face with his future; for him all was future; that is why the promise is the very essence of his faith. Moses is confronted by a present in which there culminates a previous history that is already rich with events and tradition. For Abraham the sense of the present depended solely on the future; for Moses it depends also on the past, on the given situation, the heritage received. History for him is fraught with a grandeur which faith cannot disregard, for his God is the God of a historic people, involved in precise conditions of life. The mission of Moses must take account of the sociological and psychological dimensions of the people of God; it will be his task to constitute this people as a "holy assembly", a society of believers. God's revelation to Moses has a distinctly ecclesiastical resonance.

Several features may be pointed out which illustrate this characteristic of the revelation accorded to Moses. Moses climbed Mount Sinai alone, but not for his personal edification, not as a religious genius seeking to promote his inner experiences. He went to seek in nearness to God the knowledge of the divine will which was to be conveyed to the people. In order to transform them into God's people, he went to be instructed in the commandments which would show this people how to obey their God, in the forms of the cultus which would enable them to worship without idolatry. God so effectively "descended" to save His people that He assumed the charge of their concrete moral and religious life, thus making it clear that in truth "He dwells amid the people of Israel"—an expression which occurs frequently.

The very person of Moses may be reckoned among these signs of the presence of God. The prophet served in some way as a mediator, as a link between God and the people. Like the whole cultic institution which he organizes, he in his own person makes actual for the people, and at the level of their need, the presence of the revealed God. The consequence is that when the prophet on Sinai seems to linger with his God such an absence of the sign arouses some uneasiness among them. "The people, seeing that Moses covered them with confusion by delaying to come down from the mountain, assembled around Aaron and said to him: 'Come, let us make a God who shall go before us. For as for this Moses, the man who rescued us from Egypt, we do not know what has happened to him'."[1] Thus the Israelites require another sign following the disappearance of the sign which God had given them in the person of Moses, a sign that shall go before them. The unfortunate thing is that while God can give signs that are valid, man, himself creating such signs, infringes the liberty of God, appoints places of meeting with the divine, makes for himself a God, and plunges into idolatry.

To Moses, God reveals His name; a further characteristic feature. Abraham had heard an inner voice which was self-authenticating. Pure interiority sufficed the patriarch, unaccompanied by verbal precision. The God of Moses needs to make Himself known more explicitly, for if He speaks to Moses, it is in order that Moses may speak of Him to the children of Israel. The word addressed to Moses is aimed, through him, to reach the people. Moses will have to explain himself and explain matters, surmount opposition, convince the hesitant. The immediate certitude which he has retained from his encounters with God is not transmissible as such. He must find an instrument of communication with the people, a middle term in which his faith can be conveyed in such a way as to reach the comprehension of those who are still ignorant of its essence. "If they ask me what is Thy name, what shall I answer them?" (Ex. 3:13). Such preoccupation with language marks a new stage in the

[1] Ex. 32:1. Trans. after Crampon-Bonsirven.

development.[1] God will no longer only be known through the immediate revelation of His word. He will have a name. This name will constitute, as it were, the verbal locus at which it will be possible to encounter Him, a sort of oral meeting-place granted to His people that they may approach Him. Moses must have recourse to words in order to communicate with his people. The ecclesiastical nature of his mission imparts to faith a new dimension by committing it to the way, at once perilous and fertile, of self-articulation. Moses invites reflection on the object of faith by enshrining the interior and immediate knowledge of God in an objective word.

Moreover, the mystery with which God has enshrouded Himself is not dispelled by the signs of His presence which He grants. The reply which Moses receives from God still remains obscure. Here again, man grasps something of God, but he does not apprehend God in the fullness of His being. The name both unveils and veils the One who is revealed therein. The enigmatic tetragrammaton, about whose meaning modern knowledge has not reached a sure conclusion, is typical of the mystery of that presence which does not dare to declare its name even when it names itself.

Thus, from various aspects, we see the same mediatorial technique at work. "Things" are invoked to signify the real yet mysterious presence of the God of Moses. In their various ways they reflect that polarity which we have noted in the revelation granted to Moses. Objects of this world, things, words, places even, persons too, are exalted to exercise the ambiguous function of signs. They reveal at the same time as they conceal. It becomes necessary to pierce their sig-

[1] It is true that in Gen. 17:1 we read that Yahweh addresses Abraham in these terms: "I am El-Shaddai" (God Almighty). . . . This revelation of God granted to the ageing patriarch does not contradict our remarks. As is said in Ex. 6:3: "I appeared to Abraham, Isaac, and Jacob as El-Shaddai, but by my name JHVH I did not make myself known to them." To Abraham God revealed a quality; to Moses He makes known His name, with all that the knowledge of the name implies, as a symbol of the person. It should further be noted that Gen. 17:1 belongs to the priestly tradition (P), i.e. bears Mosaic influence, thus retrospectively projected into the cycle of stories about the patriarch. This fact shows once again that the Abrahamic and Mosaic streams do not contradict each other in scripture, that they are even mingled there, the Abrahamic tradition incorporating part of Mosaism, and vice versa.

nificance and to penetrate beyond what they are in fact; it becomes necessary in a sense to "deny" them precisely in order to surpass them and to discover beyond this refusal the secret affirmation they contain.

We are here in the presence of a mediation of divine revelation—a mediation necessitated by the new dimension which Abraham's faith assumes with Moses, with whom it becomes the faith of a people, of a "holy assembly", of an *ecclesia*. First, Moses' communication with this people and subsequently the communication of the members with each other demanded that the faith should receive a new articulation.

Chapter 3

THE SPIRITUALITY OF ABRAHAM AND THE
SPIRITUALITY OF MOSES STUDIED IN CONNECTION
WITH THE OLD AND THE NEW TESTAMENTS

SUCH, then, is the complexity of Israel's faith, of which
Abraham and Moses are the two typical representative
figures on the plane of sacred history. Throughout the
whole of the Bible, according to the circumstances of the
hour and divine dispensations, this complexity recurs, at
times producing distinct and easily identifiable lines of
development, at other times indistinct when there occurs a
synthesis and harmonious balance of its complementary
elements. The difficulty lies not in recognizing the two lines
of approach; it lies rather in recognizing them without being
tempted by the facility with which the one is preferred to
the other. The critic is constantly exposed to the temptation
of reading his own predilections into the texts which he
interprets. Now our traditions, cultural and spiritual, intellectual and ecclesiastic, whether we like it or not, bring us
into line with the one or the other of the traditions of which
Abraham and Moses are the initiators and representatives in
Holy Scripture. We are predisposed to perceive and understand better whatever is related to the tradition which has
shaped our background and mental and spiritual formation.

Aware of the difficulties and limits of the undertaking, let
us try to outline some of the perspectives by which the
Biblical testimony may be organized from the points of view
defined by the two figures of Abraham and Moses.

If we are to respect the complexity of the Old Testament
revelation we must beware of the contrasting prejudices
which have warped many judgments both among protestant and catholic authors. As far as the heritage of
Moses is concerned, the fault is especially serious. Pro-

testants have the greatest difficulty in not underestimating the value of the Mosaic tradition in the corpus of revelation. They react instinctively in a negative way against every attempt to give to faith a concrete and visible expression beyond what is merely verbal. The spectre of formalism haunts their minds. This is a legitimate fear, certainly, provided it does not become an obsession which distorts realities. In particular, we may note that the Pauline polemic against the threat of Judaism and Judaic Christianity often remains, in the mentality of protestant readers of the apostle, the sole key to the understanding of the gospel. What is argued by St. Paul against the Judaic and Judaizing interpretation of the law is applied by them in the most massive way to the whole structure of the Mosaic faith. It is true that Mosaism underwent serious perversions. It may even be said that in the last analysis protestantism arose from a legitimate claim against a distortion of the Christian faith which stemmed from a false interpretation of the Mosaic factor. The sensitiveness of protestants then with regard to the risks of the Mosaic tradition is perfectly understandable, and it is easy to understand, too, that indulgence appears to them in the light of betrayal.

On the catholic side there are the same difficulties in the opposite direction. Whatever is coloured with Mosaism is sympathetically received and overvalued. Mosaic institutions are used to exempt from criticism Roman institutions. *Mutatis mutandis* they move on the same plane. The Letter to the Hebrews furnishes the credentials for a similar reading of the Old Testament as a whole, and notably when it is considered legitimate to apply to the Roman priesthood the declaration of Ps. 110: 4: "Thou art a priest for ever." On the other hand, in Roman Catholic interpretation, the spirit of prophecy is relegated to the background.

In order to respect the total balance of the component parts of Biblical revelation, it is better to set aside the famous alternative dear to the school of Wellhausen, which opposes priest and prophet. Our present-day critics do not think that there was any real opposition between these two instruments of revelation in Israel. The prophets collaborated with the priesthood, even if this collaboration led them at times to pass severe judgment on the way in which the priests understood and practised the cult; the prophets' criticism of the priesthood and the cult was constructive, its aim was to correct weaknesses and to remedy corruptions but not to dispute the basic principle. Prophets were attached to the sanctuaries. Priest and prophet constituted the two columns of the cultic edifice of Israel.

Prophecy shows itself to be the form, adapted to new circumstances, of the Abrahamic type of faith. The message of the prophet falls into history in the same way as Abraham was struck with his sense of vocation at the very beginning of the history of God's people. The prophet's word is un-expected and imperative. Nothing prepares the way for it, nothing restrains its utterance. It is the effect of a God who is bound to no contingency and who liberates man from the contingencies which bind him. Neither the graces granted, nor hallowed institutions, offer guarantees or protection. The prophet emphasizes the necessity for rupture. He is the voice of incessantly renewed demands. The past is called in question whenever piety threatens to become bogged down in it with careless ease and comfortable indifference. Faith must remain ever suspended to the word of God, which calls man today as much as yesterday. This call alone justifies history, which in consequence is never self-enclosed but de-mands of the believer an ever-renewed existence in answer to an appeal which is ever renascent. It is not only the securities of the past which undergo radical devaluation; those of the present are no less frail. The sovereignty of God must be the sole guarantee of the existence of the elect people, the sole inspiration of its politics, as of its piety. Political alliances with the heathen and religious alliances with their gods are so much adultery towards a God who shows Himself to be a husband jealous of the fidelity of His people. Faith is hope and not calculation; trust in the One who has uttered the promise, and not astute manage-ment apart from Him. At the farthest horizon of his hopes the prophet can affirm nothing other than the supreme manifestation of sovereign grace, the ultimate manifestation which will fulfil to its fullest extent the original promise implicit in the event of redemptive election. Prophetism

declares the coming of a new creation, the inconceivable but
assured inauguration of a time when the glory of God will
irradiate humanity.

To say that sacerdotal piety springs from the Mosaic intuition of God would be a mere commonplace, if no attempt
were made to throw light upon the way in which such piety
concretely expresses the basic implications of that vision of
God which Moses introduced into the stream of revelatory
history.

The God of Moses is a far-off God who reveals Himself as
distant, that is to say, who makes Himself known at the very
moment when what He makes known of Himself is precisely His grandeur, His remoteness, His mystery. The piety
inspired by such an apprehension of God will express the
paradox of a God alien to this world and yet revealed
within it. Its special dialectic will secure the balance between
these two poles, a transcendence of the world threatening
to lead to agnosticism, and a revelation within the world
which runs the risk of culminating in a confusion of the
Revealer with the earthly media of His revelation.

This difficult equilibrium is securely maintained by
sacerdotal piety through the function it assigns to mediation.
Mediation is characteristic and fundamental for Mosaic
piety. Persons and objects are made to serve the purpose of
God's self-revelation. God uses them to make known His
will and to indicate His mysterious presence. The very
keen consciousness of the extreme and terrible greatness of
God would wear away into the feeling of an inner void were
it not that the sentiment is supported by intervening media
which at one and the same time soothe it, since God emerges
from His aloofness and becomes manifest, and also foster it,
since the objects of this world, while manifesting the divine,
emphasize that God remains hidden and does not yield
Himself. The technique of sacerdotal and sacramental
mediation translates into concrete facts this exigency which
is inherent in the Mosaic type of piety. God is present
though not wholly present, as we see from the incident of
the burning bush or the theophany on Sinai. He is revealed
and He chooses men and things to convey the sense of His
presence; but He remains hidden and is irreducible to

things and men, to sacraments which signify Him and to priests who represent Him.

Such is the double culmination of that sharpened consciousness of divine transcendence which stamps the whole structure of Mosaic piety, and which is paradoxically associated with no less keen a sense of the mysterious approach of God. The Mosaic faith will endeavour to conciliate, even better, to articulate in conjunction with each other, the living intuition of the absolute transcendent majesty of God, and the further intuition of His pity, of His unfailing love. For it, God is both in heaven and on earth, beyond the world and yet in some way capable of being localized within the world. The event of election, which recalls the greatness of God, embodies itself historically. It inspires in the people the conviction that they must not become confounded with the "nations", but from this initial rupture it produces a continuity. It is less a call which casts man at every moment forward beyond himself, as was the case with Abraham; it is much more a gift which consolidates a privileged situation. It makes of Israel a holy people.

This election is reflected in stable signs, in permanent institutions, attesting the will of the God who has committed Himself to historical contingencies. Faith in the fact of election is supported by these signs. It has appointed places of meeting with God; it performs actions and utters words, it practises rites and is associated with liturgies, which are all so many means given by God to His people that they may realize, at least partially and by anticipation, that ultimate promise; so many signs and instruments of their sanctity.

Law and sacrifice; such are the two focal points of this piety characterized by the tension between the terrible transcendence of God and His gracious initiatives. In making known His will and in instituting sacrifice, the God of Moses points to His intertwined majesty and pity.

The "law" is a sign of God's condescension to dwell among His people, the formulation of the consequences of His presence at the heart of Israel. God "sanctifies" the people just as He sanctified the soil on which He was manifested to Moses (Ex. 3:5); He separates the sphere which

46

He chooses for His dwelling place, and the believer acts in accord with this. Moses took off his shoes at sight of the burning bush, the sign of God's presence; in the last analysis this gesture has the same significance as the fulfilling of the ten commandments. Ritual sanctity flows from the same source as ethical purity; both equally express the setting apart of the people by the very fact that God is present among them.

The institution of sacrifice evokes the other consequence of God's approach. God sanctifies the ground, but He burns the bush. The fire which bursts out from the bush signifies the mortal burning caused by the drawing near of God. It is in this light that we should interpret the rite of sacrifice which involves the slaying of the victim whose blood is sprinkled on the altar. God ordained this rite in order to make His people aware of what His presence in its midst implied. God's insurmountable distance from the world is reflected in this negation, this annihilation of the world. That in the first place is the truth which God conveys by the ordinance of sacrifice. However, this very transcendence is the transcendence of the Saviour God. Sacrifice also implies divine forgiveness. Just as the bush, though in flames, is not in fact consumed, so sacrifice unites to mortal burning the promise of new life. It dispenses death, and as such it induces the pious man to make an inner sacrifice. It dispenses life, and as such it enables penitent man to draw near to the living God who creates new life.

Mosaic piety goes far beyond the framework of special signs established by Moses as of divine authorization in his endeavour to mark out the path of a true cult. It is not surprising to find that priestly circles include the whole of creation in the theology of signs. To these circles are attributed those meditations, more or less speculative, from which have stemmed the texts relative to the creation of the world at the beginning of the Book of Genesis. For sacerdotal piety the cosmos became one great inclusive sign of the absolute transcendent grandeur and merciful nearness of God. God is present in the world but is not identifiable with the world. He is within His work but is at the same time irreducibly distinct from it. He is a God who is neither

47

alien to the world nor assimilable to the world. His presence assumes material objects to make of them signs and sacraments of Himself; but it remains sufficiently mysterious to reduce such objects to the status of merely enigmatic signs. Only the eye of faith can discern the flame which bursts out from the bush, faith alone can hear the hymn chanted by the heavens to the glory of their Creator.

The two types of faith which we have just identified are reflected in the New Testament. However, they are presented in quite different circumstances which we must take into account. God's new approach to humanity in Jesus Christ contains the whole substance of the prior revelation, which it carries to its perfect culmination. Nevertheless, the forms of its historical manifestation are confined within a very narrow chronological span. In comparison with the centuries during which the faith of Israel was developed and diversified, only a few decades were needed for the elaboration of the Christian faith. It must be expected that things will be less explicitly drawn out and hence less sharply contrasted.

In the person of Jesus Himself, let us note first of all that intuition characteristic of the revelation of which Abraham and the prophets have seemed to us to be the typical exponents. The gospel teaching shows Jesus as the One who is and who utters the ultimately decisive word, He to whom man must give ear, and whose message, merged with His person, makes an irruption into the history of humanity in general and of each man in particular by instituting a radically new beginning. Repentance constitutes this rupture in individual personal life, while the "fulfilment of the times" (Mk. 1:15; Gal. 4:4; Eph. 1:10) marks it in the calendar of the world. The gospel demands a radical break; the call is to receive the new wine which cannot be poured into old wineskins. Man must not look back, but forward to the coming Kingdom. From his unhappy past, his bondage, his sickness, his sin, he is delivered by the sovereign word of Jesus provided he recognizes them as the mark of his poverty and provided he is athirst for a better "righteousness". Such men, poor in spirit, and hungering and thirsting after the righteousness of the Kingdom, Jesus declares blessed. The disciple breaks all bonds; he must leave all, his affections and his wealth, after the pattern of Abraham, and following in the footsteps of his Master who has nowhere to lay His head (Mt. 8:20). He will endure hostility, like his Master (Mt. 10:16; Lk. 13:31), persecution, and even death (Mk. 8:34 and parallels). His way of life will thus stand disclosed as fully liberated from everything savouring of the heritage of this world; it will be totally dominated by the expectation of the heritage he is to receive, that heavenly treasure which God holds in store. Self-renunciation, and even the supreme self-renunciation in death, alone contains the hope of true riches, and notably of that supreme richness, the gift of eternal life (Mk. 10:28–29; Lk. 18:28–29). It is by passing through those tribulations which mark the death-agony of the old world that the disciple prepares himself for the coming of the new world.

Everything in this circle of ideas shows a prolongation of the faith of Abraham. The inner life begins with a call which was quite unforeseeable and quite unprepared for by any training or ascetic discipline. The pious are scandalized by the fact that the vocation to the Kingdom contemptuously dismisses good dispositions and religious zeal.

Divine election brings into the Kingdom those who have sprung from the seed which is the word of the sower: "Every plant which my heavenly Father has not planted will be rooted up" (Mt. 15:13). Radically based on God's sovereign and unexpected intervention, faith is open to a future which likewise depends on this sole incalculable sovereignty that must establish the Kingdom when and how it pleases. No one knows the day or the hour of its coming, and those who think they know something of the conditions of life in the Kingdom are severely reprimanded by Jesus; their remarks suffice only to show that they know neither the scriptures nor the power of God (Mk. 13:32; Mt. 24:36, 42, 50; Lk. 12:46; Mt. 25:13; Lk. 21:34; Mk. 12:24 and parallels). Man can affirm nothing, foresee nothing; all depends on the sovereign decision of God. No horizontal path leads to the Kingdom, but only a narrow gate which compels the disciple to surrender all the equipment he has

49

accumulated; he can take with him only the tiniest, the most modest of seeds, namely, the word of the promise.

Abraham is most certainly the ancestor of this faith in a God whose approach is unforeseeable, whose intervention is essentially a matter of summons and the inner sense of vocation, whose promise surpasses all the dimensions accessible to the wisdom of men. And yet, the gospel is also something else, if at any rate we do not efface from it the features which suggest another perspective.

The protestant exegete of the gospels is accustomed to stress that aspect of the teaching of Christ which prolongs the prophetic tradition and through the latter the Abrahamic faith. In that case the gospel is essentially Word and Eschatology. This convenient simplification has found so much the more credit because it has appeared to be supported by critical reflection. The exegete has considered himself justified in evaluating as posterior to Jesus whatever contained an echo of Mosaic piety, and in which could be traced the first manifestations of nascent catholicism. This type of judgment discredited as a whole all that was integral to the Mosaic tradition of faith, both from the point of view of critical authenticity and also from that of theological value.

Prudence requires a more discreet approach. It is no longer in fact possible to read the gospels in the light of either protestant or catholic presuppositions. Historically the problem is very much more complex. It has been necessary to make more flexible the pattern of influences which played upon the evolution of nascent Christianity. Judaism, Hellenism, gnosticism—to cite only the main elements of the problem—are manifested in richer and more complex forms to which we do not do justice if we remain confined to the alternative, catholicism or protestantism. The frontiers of historical probability have been shifted. Today we can look more calmly and dispassionately at a page of the New Testament in which there is affirmed a piety of the Mosaic type, without feeling ourselves obliged at once to suspect in it a latent germ of catholicism. Today judgments concerning authenticity are possible which fifty years ago would have classed a man among the ignorant.

Indeed, we must recognize that the gospel of Jesus Christ is the object of two types of exegetical approach. It is unnecessary to dwell here on the exegesis of Abrahamic inspiration, which emphasizes that the gospel is the word of summons, the preaching of the good news, the appeal to the rupture involved in repentance, the proclamation of forgiveness, the expectation of the eschatological Kingdom. On the other hand it must be emphasized that the exegesis of Mosaic inspiration insists on the affirmation that the Word became flesh. This leads it to throw into prominence the acts of Jesus, to stress the insertion of the divine into the human, the communication of grace by resort to concrete means which affect man on the level of his real humanity. The divinity of Jesus is revealed not only in His teaching but also in His acts, which are not so much concrete illustrations of His teaching as manifestations of His power which embodies that teaching on the plane of the concrete and fleshly.

The Mosaic reading of the gospel also brings to light the tension between inaccessible divine transcendence and the historic communication of grace. Jesus pardons and heals at one and the same time. He does not merely pronounce an absolution which will bear eschatological fruits; He restores the creature here and now; He inaugurates in this present economy of existence an order of new life. His word is not merely a summons in view of what is to come; it creates in the present a new historical fact. It is something else besides a promise; it is the actuality of the kingly rule of God, who has really drawn near to men in the person of the supreme Bearer of graces which God wills to embody in history for the salvation of mankind. If need arose it was sufficient to touch the mere hem of His garment to be healed (Mt. 9:20; Lk. 8:44), and His sole presence in a house permitted Him to say that salvation had entered it (Lk. 19:9).

What God has given in Jesus Christ He does not withdraw; He does not erase from history what He has written within it. Salvation has entered the world to pursue within it its beneficent effects. In a sense the incarnation continues. Moses, like Abraham, was far-seeing, but his vision took as its point of departure the present reality of divine graces and he foresaw the future economy as something integrally linked to the historical continuity of the work of salvation. The promise thus assumed a concrete consistency in sociological and liturgical forms. Similarly, the eschatology which forms the far-off horizon in the preaching of Jesus does not blot out the intermediate period which separates the present from that ultimate future. Jesus chooses men who will extend and prolong His action; and alike the message with which He entrusts them, and the powers with which He invests them, exalt them above their personal condition of life, so much so that Jesus tells them that he who receives them receives in effect Himself (Mt. 10:40). They will heal as He has healed; they will forgive as He has forgiven; they will communicate His powerful and soul-saving presence. The work of salvation will be continued by these beings of flesh and blood to whom the Lord promises His presence for the accomplishment of their task (Mt. 28:18–20). The Holy Spirit will actualize this divine presence after the resurrection.

The Mosaic faith feels with special acuteness the paradoxical polarity of the mystery of God. The God of Moses came down into this world to save, but He also enters into contradiction with it: He reveals Himself as the flame which devours but does not consume. We have seen how the sacrificial system prescribed by the Mosaic law makes manifest this polarity. So it is with the passion of Jesus, the sacrifice of Jesus. This is no tragic accident of history, it is not the consequence of a painful misunderstanding. The passion of Christ is necessary; Jesus says that the Son of Man "must" suffer and be rejected of men. The approach of God cannot fail to set alight, on the level of the realities of this world, that fire of which Jesus said that He came to kindle it (Lk. 12:49); an enigmatic saying which is explained if we remember that the approach of God already of old caused the bush to flame with fire and hurled lightnings on Mount Sinai. This symbolical language suggests the decisive tension set up in the world by the approach or the presence of God. Of this tension the cross is the ultimate example and the permanent sign. It perpetuates for ever the teaching implicit in the sacrifices of the old covenant.

God must destroy the "world" precisely in order to give it life; the "world" cannot receive life except by means of death-bringing suffering and trial.

There is great profit in comparing with the Mosaic traditions the explanation which Jesus gave of His own sacrifice in the upper room. The "impossible" encounter between God and the world gives rise to a conflict, a crisis, kindles a devouring fire, brings death in its train; but this encounter is of saving significance for the world; God reveals Himself, the fire does not consume, the blood of the victim is the symbol of the new life which God grants; after the cross comes the event of the resurrection. If we bear in mind this understanding of things we can readily enter into the perspective outlined by Jesus in His declaration concerning the bread which He distributes to His disciples: "This is my body." This enigmatic explanation of His sacrifice brings out the paradoxical truth that the sacrifice does not spell in the last resort a destruction of life, but implies rather the life-giving action of God beyond death. The fire did not consume the bush! God had effectively made Himself present by fire. Presence but not localization. A presence which devours from within the sign which it takes, but without consuming the outward properties of the latter.

It is the characteristic essence of the Mosaic faith, which is here carried to its supreme expression, to seize in the things of this world, in carnal realities, that burning presence which transforms them into instruments of salvation. The Johannine comparison between the cross and the fiery serpent which Moses lifted up in the wilderness might serve to illustrate this same theme in yet another manner (Jn. 3:14) and still within the Mosaic perspective.

The Mosaic aspect of the gospel faith is again apparent in those texts where an ecclesiastical concern emerges. The gospel is not merely the word which summons to repentance and faith, the word which proclaims forgiveness and announces the coming of the Kingdom. It is, further, the good news of a life lived in brotherly love in the communion of those who are gathered together in the name of their Master and between whom the presence of this Master constitutes a bond which both assumes and surpasses their individualities. They form a "little flock" because, having a common Shepherd, they share in one and the same divine Presence. The evangelist Matthew has particularly emphasized in numerous texts this communal and ecclesial aspect of the gospel which closely links to the people of Israel this new people of God. His preoccupation with this point of view is disclosed, above all, in the use which he makes of the word *ecclesia*, a word which he alone uses and in fact uses twice over, notably in the version which he gives of the conversation of Jesus with the disciples on the road to Caesarea Philippi (Mt. 16:13–20).

The scene which here unfolds itself is a sort of replica of the scene centred on the burning bush in Horeb. In both cases God is concerned with the same thing, although the circumstances are different: He wishes to consolidate His people, to group them into a "holy assembly", a *qa'al*, an *ecclesia*. In either case He commissions a man to undertake special responsibilities with regard to this people: Moses and Peter receive a special mission which sets them apart from the rest of their brothers. The task which they have to fulfil includes, in particular, the making known of the name of Him who has revealed Himself to them. Yahweh made Himself known to Moses as the God of Abraham, of Isaac, and of Jacob, as the God of Israel. In parallelism, God reveals to Peter that Jesus is the Christ. It is in the name of these revelations that Moses and Peter bind into a community the believers who are entrusted to their charge. As the task awaiting them exceeds their strength, a promise of special help, in both cases, intervenes to overcome the hesitations justified by so difficult a mission. Many centuries later, the apostle Peter pursues in favour of the new Israel the mission which formerly had devolved on Moses.

The coexistence of the two theological structures which we have identified up to this point is manifestly continued in the rest of the New Testament, in various guises, as we might expect. Each of the Biblical witnesses gives in his own way, and with more or less partiality or clarity, some glimpse of the complex and mysterious wealth hidden in the Christ.

First, the great figure of the apostle Paul imposes itself

on our attention. To be sure, St. Paul has become the great patron of the theology of the Word which falls from a height on man; the whole of Pauline theology and spirituality may be understood in the light of the incident on the Damascus road. Paul is likewise the herald of justification by faith to the exclusion of the works of the law. He is pre-eminently the "charismatic" apostle, the man who was snatched from his past by a crushing break and guided towards the adventures of faith by the overruling commands of the Spirit. He extols prophecy in the church and seems to attach little importance to sacerdotal functions or established authorities. Against the latter he does not hesitate to insist on his personal freedom. He seems to commit the communities which he founds and organizes exclusively to the spontaneity of the gifts of the Spirit. "Word", "faith", and "spirit" might be taken as summing up this portrait of the apostle to the Gentiles—a portrait which makes of him the heir of the faith of Abraham. We have already noted what degree of importance he himself attributes to the figure of the patriarch, the very type of the believer justified by faith, the bearer of those promises by which Israel lived and which the Christian church inherited.

Such is St. Paul, at least the Paul whom almost the whole protestant world carries in its heart, the Paul whom protestants find reflected in the letters, especially in those which they read in preference to the others. It is, of course, to this Paul that they refer to justify their own theological positions and their own type of spirituality. This Paul exists, evidently; but he is not the only Paul. For the apostle has indeed another face, less familiar to protestant readers. The Letters to the Romans and to the Galatians do not constitute the whole of his work.

Catholic exegetes are better prepared than their protestant colleagues to pierce the significance of certain of the essential themes developed in the Letters to the Corinthians, the Colossians, and the Ephesians. Their dogmatic tradition has made them more perceptive of the realities of church and sacramental life which lie behind these documents, and they feel more at ease in the passages which Paul devotes to such subjects. What in the eyes of protestants seems to be no more than a simple allusion assumes in the view of catholics a density of meaning rich with extensive dogmatic implications. Hence they on their side are menaced by the temptation to read into these texts a wealth of suggestions which certainly exceeds the objective content, as do also protestants when they read the Letters to the Romans and to the Galatians.

It is clear that the group of letters to which we are now referring has a much more familiar ring in the ears of catholic readers than in those of protestant readers. Let us recall only the rarity of the word *ecclesia* in the Letters to the Galatians and to the Romans, as contrasted with the frequency of its occurrence in the other letters in question, and let us bear in mind also to what an extent the importance of the idea surpasses the frequency of the word. We might note further that no mention is made of the Lord's Supper in the Letters to the Romans and to the Galatians, whereas the first Letter to the Corinthians treats the theme not merely in relation to church life but also against the background of the sacrifices of the old covenant. Is it not in fact interesting to note that Paul illuminates the character of the eucharist by drawing a comparison with the sacrificial rites of the Mosaic law? Hence it is on the sacrificial doctrine of Mosaism that he draws in order to interpret the meaning of the death of Jesus. Paul did not make a total and sharp break with Moses, as is too often believed. He reacted rather, and above all, against the interpretation of Mosaism given by the scribes and Pharisees.

Thus it is not really permissible to represent Paul as a purely charismatic personality, and to make of him the first protestant! The polarity of Biblical faith is to be found in him as in his Master and Lord, Jesus Christ. The texts would supply copious proofs of this. We will content ourselves with adducing two further examples. The formula—so characteristic of Pauline spirituality—of "being in Christ" still often remains puzzling to us because we wish to reduce it to one single meaning. In fact, it reflects the polarity of the apostle's faith. On the one hand, it expresses the individual and immediate relation of the believer to his Lord, a relation which rests on the sole sufficiency of the gospel of the cross and of faith. On the other hand, it expresses the ecclesial situation of the believer as incorporated in the body of Christ, the fact of belonging to the visible church and the solidarity which exists among the church's members. The one meaning may not be sacrificed to the other; Paul thinks of both at one and the same time. Likewise the idea of the apostolate illustrates the polarity of the Pauline faith: the apostolate is both a charismatical function, validated by the content of the preaching, that is to say, by the Christ speaking through the mouth of His witness, and also a function instituted by the Lord, an office which does not depend on the men who assume it.

We must discontinue our search through the scriptures. Yet a few indications are necessary in regard to Johannine theology, by reason of its great importance in the whole field of scriptural testimony.

In the Fourth Gospel the tension between revelation and history is seen at its most acute, while at the same time it is deliberately overcome by the thought of the author. The whole gospel is constructed on the basis of the antithesis *Logos-Sarx*, and Jesus in His person assumes the unity of this pair of opposites. As in the case of the Abrahamic faith, the Word is the constitutive element in the process of revelation; but the special characteristic of the Johannine Word is that it is not an inner event but an objective action of God, a manifestation of God in concrete realities, in "flesh". Transcendence has entered history; He who was from the beginning with God, and shared with God the status of divinity, has taken on the conditions of human life. There results from this incarnation an ambiguous situation which at once and directly recalls that of the burning bush; the reality that is seen is the man "Jesus, the son of Joseph, whose father and mother we know" (Jn. 6:42). But the reality which is thus seen is not the whole of the reality, any more than is the word spoken by His lips the whole of the Word. Faith is necessary if we are to see the flame set ablaze the bush, and faith is again necessary if we are to see in the son of Joseph the Son of God and to understand that His words are Spirit and Life, that they are the words of eternal life (Jn. 6:63–68).

Reality is what it is, but at the same time it is something else, because the Logos has "come down"; this is the central theme in Johannine theology and it recalls Yahweh's word to Moses: "I have come down . . ." The approach of God is at one and the same time manifested and concealed in this self-contradictory reality. The believer beholds in Jesus the effulgent glory (Jn. 1:14), whereas the unbeliever is blind to this light which, however, shines brightly at the heart of darkness (Jn. 1:4–5). It is understandable why the Gospel according to St. John presents the unfolding of the ministry of Jesus as an uninterrupted succession of misunderstandings. Everything in it has a double meaning; faith seizes the real meaning of what Jesus says and does, while "the Jews" who personify unbelief fail to understand either the words or the deeds of the Messiah. Revelation is so truly embodied in the sphere of the concrete that it gives rise to an interpretation that is pedestrian, even coarse or ridiculous, as for example when it is a question of the new birth (3:3), of the new temple (2:20), of the water (4:15), or of the "flesh" which the Son of Man gives to eat (6:52), etc. The words remain, but they are burnt from within by the revelation which they convey; they radiate for the believer the glory which indwells them. It would be necessary to quote the whole gospel to illustrate this. Amphibology is here exalted to the dignity of bearing witness to faith.

This amounts to saying that the Fourth Gospel is akin to the Mosaic stream of revelation through its concern to show the actualization of meta-history within history. The polarity of faith, stretched as it is between its heavenly origin and its earthly form, is emphasized on every page. Must we further remind the reader that this gospel paradoxically offers a powerful synthesis of mystical individualism and church sacramentalism? In the eyes of protestant readers it appears to be the most "spiritual", the most charismatic of the gospels, the most pietistic, the most individualistic; it is the gospel which speaks of worship "in spirit and in truth", of the "words which are spirit and life", of the immediate presence of Christ with His own through the promised Comforter, etc. The catholic reader, however, notices how careful is this gospel to point out the concrete conditions

58

of this communion, its insistence on baptism, the eucharist, the unity of the church. Those pages which amplify these themes, minimized by protestants, are the spiritual food of catholics.

The same intuition of divine transcendence leads to other points of affinity between Mosaic spirituality and the Fourth Gospel. For Moses, revelation assumed a certain externality of character. The senses were in some way made use of to enable man to apprehend something of the invisible mystery of the Godhead. We noted that it suggested a mingling of both the possibility and the impossibility of seeing God, this being the reflection and the result of the paradoxical move of a God who has "come down" from heaven, according to the word declared to Moses, in order to place Himself on man's level. The whole of Johannine theology is similarly centred on the invisibility of God—"No one has ever seen God" (Jn. 1:18; 6:46; 1 Jn. 4:12)—but nevertheless God has made Himself visible by the coming of the Logos in the form of flesh: "We have beheld His glory" (Jn. 1:14), "he who has seen me has seen the Father" (Jn. 14:9; 12:45). To behold the glory of the Son is to behold the glory of the Father and thus has been granted that prayer of Moses: "Show me Thy glory" (Ex. 33:18). The mere sight of the bronze serpent had saving value: "And if a serpent bit any man, he would look at the bronze serpent and live" (Num. 21:9). The gospel interweaves the episode into its own texture. To see the one who is lifted up, such is the condition of salvation for Johannine faith; the Son of Man must be lifted up that man may see Him and believe on Him in order to be saved (Jn. 3:14; 8:28; 6:62; 12:32). It is not sight alone that is brought into play by Johannine spirituality; we are indeed surprised by the emphasis with which the Johannine Christ speaks of His flesh that man must eat (in 6:54 the text does not use the word φάγω but τρώγω, which refers to eating by animals, or by man when raw foods are in question); similarly we are astonished to read in 1 Jn. 1:1 the detail concerning "that which we have touched with our hands". We have here a realism which is all the more striking because found in a highly spiritual and mystical context. Johannine spirituality is centred on a

word, but a word which was incarnated, "that which we
have seen and heard" (1 Jn. 1:3).

These echoes of the Mosaic faith in the Fourth Gospel
cannot all be pointed out. The Christ Logos "has set up His
tabernacle among us", says John (1:14), in which we
recognize an allusion to the tabernacle which God caused to
be set up in Israel that He might dwell among His people
(Ex. 29:45). The declaration of Jn. 5:46 is explicit: "If you
believed Moses, you would believe me, for he wrote of me."
The Johannine narratives have drawn of the Christ a
portrait that is polarized, and in which the tension between
the transcendent Logos and the incarnate Logos is sharply
underlined. He who was with the Father, in the heavenly
glory, remains a terrible mystery even in His incarnation.
Just as one could not touch, without being struck, that holy
mountain on which the God of Moses descended, so one cannot place a profane hand on the Johannine Christ without
recoiling in mortal fear (Jn. 18:6). But again, he who had
access to the terrible God of Sinai could enjoy with Him an
intimacy of converse such as a man enjoys with his friend;
so too the disciples of the Christ were called by Him no
longer His servants but His friends (Jn. 15:15). Finally—
not to become prolix in enumerating these points of affinity—
how can we refrain from noting that the God of Moses
reveals Himself under the name of "I am" (Ex. 3:14;
"Say this to the people of Israel, I AM has sent me to you").
The spirituality of Moses is prolonged in the effort made by
the Johannine faith to grasp in its turn by means of reflection, and to crystallize in words, what has been revealed to it
of the mystery of God in Christ. Whence the first Christo-
logical definitions of the prologue, and the declarations in
which the Christ Himself defines His own being by saying:
"I am . . . " ($\dot{\epsilon}\gamma\dot{\omega}$ $\epsilon\dot{\iota}\mu\iota$). The same movement of faith is
found in both contexts. In making known His name, the
God of Moses localizes Himself, if one may dare to use the
expression; He in some way encloses His being within a
word, in verbal flesh, in a carnal word. The presence of the
Logos in history constitutes the ultimate term of that descent
of the God of Moses to the level of the most concrete and
tangible of human realities.

Chapter 4

THE CHARACTERISTICS OF THE SPIRITUALITY OF
ABRAHAM AND OF THE SPIRITUALITY OF MOSES

T HE two streams of inspiration, springing from Abraham
and Moses respectively, at every point overflow the
typical personages of the patriarch, the father of
believers, and of the prophet, the political and religious
leader who laid the foundations of the life of the elected
people. We are here confronted by two styles of piety, two
spiritualities, two mentalities, each bearing its essential
character, each implying an emotional and mental universe
proper to itself. The history of the Christian church may be
envisaged from the point of view of the coexistence, sometimes peaceful, sometimes stormy, of these two ways of
reading scripture, the one favouring the heritage of Abraham, the other the heritage of Moses; it being unfortunately
apparent that their fruitful co-operation is difficult and rare.

Before following outside the pages of the New Testament
the destiny of these two inheritances, let us attempt to characterize them with greater precision. The faith of Abraham
and the faith of Moses are the same faith. It is the God of the
patriarchs who reveals Himself to Moses, and Moses is
aware of this (Ex. 3:6). But the very circumstances of the
revelation granted to these two heralds of God already suggest why it is that the same God makes Himself known to
them from different angles of approach, and why each will
apprehend in a different way the unique object of their
faith.

On the one hand, with Abraham, we are present at the
first springing up of faith. It is a question here of an
absolute beginning. Faith avers itself as an immediate and
essentially inner certitude, a word which the believer hears
within the depths of his being, and which is irresistibly and

61

absolutely self-evidencing to him. To call this word in question would be to cease to hear it. It is what it is in the very act which receives it. It did not exist, under any form whatsoever, before manifesting itself in the secret depths of the being which receives it. Its total and absolute actuality also means that it remains what it is only if it is heard anew in the same act which already at the first made it actual. Hence this faith renews itself from moment to moment; its continuity consists in this incessant self-renewal. If it could have a continuity which did not consist in its own self-renewal it would survive as a memory of itself, just as the absent one survives in the letters which he leaves after his departure. Thus the Abrahamic faith finds itself constantly called in question by its own very nature, and so as not to be perverted. The sacrifice of Isaac, as we have seen, illustrates this necessity for the faith of Abraham to place itself ever anew before a real new beginning—the necessity always to begin afresh.

If such is the condition of the Abrahamic faith, it is because, on the level of the inner experience of the believer, it is the effect of the self-revelation of the God who gives life to the dead and summons into existence that which has no being. This is the formulation proposed by the apostle Paul when he wishes to characterize the God of the Christian faith seen in its Abrahamic aspect (cf. Rom. 4:17). In piety of the Abrahamic type, God reveals Himself as He who "falls" from a height and unexpectedly into a situation which He radically unhinges and changes, to such an extent that His intervention constitutes a real creative act, a resurrection of the dead to life. The way in which the apostle expresses himself is highly significant. It cannot be more strongly suggested that in such cases God reveals Himself as the One who acts with sovereign authority, as the source of all efficacious power, who executes and, in so doing, summons into existence. He is the God who intervenes so that that which is not, may be. He is the God who introduces into the present, regarded as the term of the past, that element of newness which makes it pregnant with the future and a veritable inauguration of a new epoch of time. In Biblical terms, He is the God of the promise, for the promise is precisely that fructifying seed which henceforth separates the present from the past to orientate it dynamically towards its future.

Abrahamic "theology", that is to say, doctrine of God, will therefore place at its centre the affirmation of the liberty of God, since, moreover, this liberty is both the form in which the sovereign intervention of his God is manifested to the believer and also the very condition of divine sovereignty. God owes nothing to anyone, it might be said. He is free because His action depends only on Himself. Nor does God ask anything of anyone, we might go on to assert. He is free because His action has the nature of a gift; it is gracious by definition, since it is creative from the starting point of nothingness, life-giving from the starting point of death.

Confronted by this God, man cannot but become aware of the weakness of his condition. The spirituality engendered by the revelation of the God who is sovereign and free will be dominated by the consciousness of the impotence of man as contrasted with the divine promise and action. Such is the situation of Abraham confessing his "necrosis". God discloses Himself as the God of the promise only to him who makes no claim to take the place of God or even merely to collaborate with God in the accomplishment of what is essentially God's own work. Faith is the act of self-surrender to, of self-abandonment to, the gracious intervention of God. It is even more: it means recognizing that the intervention of grace is substantially creative of new life, and that there is absolute break of continuity between the old being which lived in unawareness of the promise and the new being brought to birth by revelation. Grace is more than a healing power: it is the grace of the God of Abraham who gives life to the dead and creates out of nothingness; by definition it excludes man from its operation and itself accomplishes all. The Abrahamic believer avows his radical incapacity.

Thus the faith of the Abrahamic type lives in and by the certitude that the sovereignty of grace suffices for all that is necessary to the achievement of salvation. It cannot fail to set aside any idea of man's co-operation in the work of redemption. To live fully in the total dimension and reality of the promise, it annihilates every human pretension, what Paul described as the καύχημα.

The same movement of thought which causes the whole efficacy of grace to be attributed to God's action alone, likewise attributes to grace alone the initiative of the divine action. The God of Abraham is the God of absolute beginnings. If He acts, it is without taking counsel of anyone, it is apart from any movement external to Himself. Abrahamic piety will foster at its heart the secret contemplation of the mystery of its origins and of the freedom of God. "One will be taken and the other left," said Jesus (Mt. 24:40–41), and St. Paul in his turn reminds us that Isaac was loved and Esau rejected (Rom. 9:13).

The word will play a central part in the Abrahamic type of piety, for the idea of the word satisfies several of its fundamental requirements. It is as the Author of the Word that the God who intervenes with sovereign freedom makes Himself known, for the spoken word is pre-eminently that act which manifests the person apart from all contingent relations. He who is sovereign is he who has the power of the word, who speaks or is silent, and when he speaks, the thing is done; the man who has not the power of the word, who has not the right to speak, has virtually lapsed from the dignity of his human status: he is reduced to the level of an animal or a robot.

The word is again the expression of a sovereignty which lays in the present the bases of future reality. The word of the sovereign is the seed of the future. It declares today what will be effected tomorrow, what it will accomplish tomorrow in virtue of its own inherent efficacy. That is why it is essentially of the nature of a "promise". The importance of the idea of the promise in the perspective of Abrahamic piety is basically justified, and for the same reason as that for which the gospel likens the word of God to the seed of the sower.

The word is, further, the supreme instrument of sovereignty as a living force, exercised and experienced. It is when he hears the sovereign speak that the subject becomes most fully conscious of his subjection. The word of the sovereign disposes of him, and not only of his body, but (theoretically at least) of his soul also; it enjoins him not merely to obey but to agree, not merely to submit but to accept. It is through the word that tyranny succeeds in its purposes of enslavement, whether in such cases it is called propaganda or psychological pressure, and it is then that the tongue becomes the worst of evils (cf. Jas. 3).

But in other ways the word is the best of things, when it is brought into the service of a sovereignty which uses it for the good of the person addressed. For the word gives occasion for the word of response, and thus is born dialogue, which begins with an inner dialogue. It is in face of a word which summons him that man first becomes fully conscious of himself. Then arises that secret debate in which response is prepared, that self-conscious reflection upon himself in which man questions himself, descends into the depths of his own being so as to become aware of himself at the deepest level that he may commit himself as a responsible creature in face of the summons of conscience.

We see, then, why the faith of Abraham assigns fundamental importance to the word. It is within a pattern of relations determined by the word that the relation between the person of the sovereign God and the person of the believer can most adequately be realized. We see also why the faith of Abraham becomes the educator of conscience. It implies this capacity for response, it makes its appeal to a person who is *respons-ible*. An instrument in the service of God's sovereignty, the word does not stifle the liberty of man, which it in fact creates rather than destroys.

Poised by his faith in an attitude of dependence towards the God who addresses him, the Abrahamic believer orientates his being in its fullest depth towards the future, towards that which the promise declares. He lives in expectation. His faith is nourished by hope. At every moment he clings to what he will receive from God, not to what he may already have received. The graces granted are not graces acquired. The action of God imposes itself on his attention by its ever-fresh accessions. Neither the past nor the present are for faith disposable, utilizable realities which might constitute the believer in an autonomy at least relative, might absolve him from the need to receive each time afresh his daily spiritual bread. Were it not always expected and hence always future, the action of grace would become confused with the "world". The supremacy of the promise requires that it shall always be "beyond". To the extent that it lives by the revelation of the promise, faith is essentially eschatological. What God has already done is only a token of what He will do and not even a warrant. Faith could not become stabilized in that past without the adulteration of idolatry, for it would in so doing confound the marks of an absence with presence itself and the hot ashes with the fire.

In this tension towards a promise which transcends each one of its earthly fulfilments there lies an unremitting effort to reject continuity and consolidation. Abraham lived out the faith of the nomad which he was; his God cannot be confounded with anything of what exists, nor with anything of what He grants. He is, only in the act of His speaking. His word actualizes His promise and realizes His presence. He is not present in what He has said, but in what He says. He is not a God who has ceased to speak, but a God who speaks. When faith translates this dynamic, actual, and present word in terms borrowed from human speech it can give but a clumsy, distorted, inadequate idea of it, in the last analysis a mere dead letter. The word of God is received in faith as a manifestation of power, an act. When God speaks He acts, and His action always transcends what man can convey in language, what God has said. The faith of an Abraham refuses to find support in the traces left by the living word of God in human speech; it disowns the constructions which reason might build on the words which reflect its inner certitude.

Hence faith of the Abrahamic type tends to remove any confusion of the word of the promise with anything human, earthly, factual, historical. It aims at pure interiority. The action of God cannot be stabilized, localized, represented, since it remains ever transcendent. God is nowhere, except in the act itself of His revelatory intervention, that is, in what He says when He summons a soul. There is only one temple worthy of Him, that is the sphere where His word is heard and received; in other words, the heart of the believer. One does not encounter God by entering into some sacred area; one encounters Him by listening to Him: faith is born of hearing (Rom. 10:17). The sole place in which God dwells is the hearts of His people; His only house is where His children are, a spiritual edifice built of living stones (1 Pet. 2:5).

The fundamental unity which binds the faith of Abraham to that of Moses does not, as we have already seen, involve a uniformity in the two types of revelation of which these two great figures are the bearers.

The conditions in which Moses apprehended the revelation of which he was the object clearly indicate its basic character. This revelation brings into play a bush, a mountain, and a storm. One must pierce the symbol to divine its underlying meaning and be able to read the intention which lies beyond the external setting. We must, however, in the first place emphasize the character of externality which marks this revelation. Unlike the word addressed to Abraham which reached the patriarch directly in the secret depths of his conscience, without the use of any intermediary whatsoever, here is a word which has recourse to mediation through external things. Moses' attention is awakened and he becomes involved through facts which are expressed in the sphere of concrete realities. The word of Abraham's God is purely interior; this God is present because He speaks, He is present in His word, and His word is supported by nothing and leaves no trace. The God of Moses is revealed by means of instruments which are raised to the dignity of efficacious signs, and these instruments subsist independently of that act of speaking which they signify, which they both herald and recall.

On closer inspection, this mode of revelation is organically bound to the very nature of the Mosaic revelation. If the spirituality of the Abrahamic type stems from an intuition of the sovereign freedom of the God who establishes the absolute beginnings required by Biblical faith, the spirituality typified by Moses springs rather from an intuition of the compassionate faithfulness of the God who pursues the work begun so that the ends implied in His initiatives may be attained. Abraham was the first, and his faith bears the stamp of the necessities involved in absolute beginnings; it implies divine freedom and sovereignty. Moses comes after; he enters into an undertaking already in course of execution, into a project already embodied in history; he receives a heritage, and his task will be to ensure its continued operation in new conditions. The faith of Moses bears the stamp of fidelity to the initial plan, of the need to adapt its forms to circumstances. It is thus that the God of Abraham reveals Himself to Moses as the God whose faithfulness pursues through the developments of history the realization of the initial promise, and pursues it by "coming down" to the unhappy children of Israel so as to express His steadfast love in the form demanded by new times.

If above we could schematize the faith of Abraham by saying that its object was the action of a free and sovereign God, and that sovereignty was the "matter" of the action as freedom was its "form", here we can schematize the faith of Moses by saying that its object is the action of a pitying and faithful God and that pity is the "matter" of the action, just as fidelity is its "form". The Abrahamic believer is perceptive, above all, of the divine initiative, of the fact that it is God who lays the basis of absolute and true beginnings. The faith of Moses has special insight into the fact of continuity, the fact that God enters into the horizontal process of history, and that His pity manifests His fidelity by embodying that fidelity in the very contingent and relative realities of this world.

Moses enters into an unfolding historical process. What Abraham glimpsed as a promise, Moses contemplates as a reality. The faith of Abraham could rest its gaze only on the eschatological horizon of history; the faith of Moses can consider what God is granting and accomplishing in token of His compassionate fidelity to His promises. The very reality of this people whom God calls "my people" is in itself a fulfilment of the promise and a sign of the divine fidelity. God cannot separate His own fate from that of His people. Their suffering causes Him to suffer, and that is why He does not remain outside time and space—the sphere wherein is enacted the destiny of this people which is His own: He comes down, He makes His presence known in time and space, so that He might deliver His people. The basic intuition of Moses has as its object the God who comes to help and save, the God of deliverance, the merciful God (Ex. 33:19; 34:6). There will be a people in the midst of whom God will dwell, a place which will be the place of meeting appointed by Him whose name is mercy, that faith may realize that He is ever the One who has come down. God sets Abraham apart to make of him a great nation; He has also set apart His people in whose midst He establishes His dwelling place. The nearness of this God who has "come down", His presence in this visible world, hallowed the ground on which Moses saw the bush aflame. Rudimentary as is this idea of the sacred—and with it must be compared the other manifestations, notably the mount of Sinai or the ark of the covenant (cf. Ex. 19:11–12 and *passim*)—it conveys in very concrete terms the Mosaic sensitiveness to the presence of the God who has "come down" from heaven in order to rescue His people. The initial election of which Abraham was the object thus assumed an embodiment on the historical level; in a sense—and this it will be easy to misunderstand—the event of election is here being endowed with earthly concrete shape; henceforth it will be linked by the redemptive plan of God to certain realities of this "world".

The fact that election is thus becoming woven into the horizontal process of history results in a certain shift of emphasis as regards the idea of promise and covenant. For the Abrahamic faith, it is the promise which counts, which is basic, for the promise constitutes the concrete form that election takes. To the extent that the faith of Abraham assigns a part to the idea of the covenant, it understands the latter as the self-commitment which God unilaterally assumes through the promise which He makes and which He will fulfil. The theology of Moses understands election much more concretely; election is the choice of a particular people, and the covenant constitutes the charter of this people as the elected people. The "descent" of God creates new conditions for the realization of the plan which the promise proclaimed. The sanctification of the people whom God has delivered from bondage that He might make among them His dwelling place, commits this people in relationship to this God. The presence of God in its midst obliges and qualifies Israel to accomplish certain tasks. The promise is now embodied in a particular covenant, and the covenant involves historical man. Obedience of the Abrahamic type implies an attitude of passivity in regard to the sovereign action of God; the believer must recognize his own "necrosis" so that God may fulfil His promise. But the obedience of the Mosaic type implies an attitude of activity, by reason of the need to honour the covenant; for obedience to the covenant is the condition of the fulfilling of the promise. "Choose whom you wish to serve . . ." The alternative is characteristic of Moses. Abraham could not choose; he was chosen. Election is unilateral; covenant bilateral. The part which the covenant assigns to the people opens up a new perspective; man makes his entry into theology, for he is sanctified by the presence of God.

Sustained as it is by the revelation of a God who approaches this world and uses it in order to make Himself known, the spirituality of Moses will be aware of the cosmos as integrally connected with faith. Since God uses visible things as signs of His mysterious presence, they are therefore at His service and command. God can draw near because He is not alien to this world. The note of pure interiority which characterizes the spirituality of Abraham cannot support itself by reference to any object drawn from this world. The faith of Moses, on the contrary, shows no repugnance to exalting the world in its totality to the dignity of a sign of the presence of God. We have already reminded the reader that the speculations relative to creation, to which the first lines of the Book of Genesis bear witness, emerged from priestly circles. This is understandable. It was indeed necessary at last to justify the paradoxical affirmation of faith that the transcendent and invisible God had revealed Himself by enshrining His presence within the sphere of the historical and visible. The doctrine of creation safeguarded at one and the same time these two affirmations of faith: God is not confounded with the cosmos, and yet the cosmos stands in the closest relation to God. In a world totally alien to Him, the God of Moses would not have been able to "come down".

Among the external signs by which the faith of Moses apprehends something of the presence of its God, we must also cite the fact of human language.

Like the God of Abraham, the God of Moses reveals Himself by means of a word; He engages a dialogue; He calls that He might have a reply; He treats man as a *respons-ible* being, as has been said above. Nevertheless, this word is here otherwise expressed. It is related to a reality external to man's inner conscience; it is no longer the purely interior word which was heard by Abraham. The voice of God resounds with the terrible accents of thunder on Mount Sinai or is distinguished in the lambent fire which plays about the burning bush. The words heard or uttered will assume a certain importance; external, they will be capable of becoming independent. In their turn they will take on the status of signs, able to intimate something valid about the presence of God. Abraham could be satisfied to listen. Moses must learn to speak, and God teaches him in fact to speak a word which will express all; He reveals to him His name. The faith of Moses has at its command words which are efficacious signs. In the structure of his faith speech of this kind acquires a positive function. How should we be surprised at this, since language is built up from knowledge of the world and since faith finds in the world an intimation of the Creator God? God can "come down" in the language of man in order to signify His presence just as He can come down on Mount Sinai or in the burning bush: in either case, He is at home, among His own. Hence it will be possible and legitimate, in the eyes of the Mosaic believer, after having heard God speak, to speak of God, to speak on the subject of God, to admit that language is efficacious to enlighten, that it can to a certain extent elucidate the inner and immediate data of faith by the examination and use of words in the processes of thought.

Nevertheless, no sort of external thing (including speech), nothing in fact of what is used as an earthly support for the Mosaic faith, assumes the function in a simple and direct way. The God who has come down remains the hidden God. The signs which He vouchsafes remain only signs. Everything by which God reveals Himself is basically and deeply ambiguous. God reveals Himself in the bush, but He is not the bush. When He speaks to Moses the people hear only the terrible roar of the tempest; God speaks in the thunder and lightning, but the thunder and lightning are not the word of God. Faith must pierce the external data and penetrate beyond the veil, as in the temple, where the presence of God is accessible only when faith has been able to realize that God lies beyond all that is visible or sensuously apprehensible. Similarly on Sinai, Moses encountered God only when passing into the thick cloud which concealed from him every earthly object. Then, no longer seeing anything, he succeeded in seeing the invisible.

The faith of Moses verifies the second half of the definition of faith given in the Letter to the Hebrews; it sees what is invisible as though it were visible, because simultaneously it affirms and immediately denies that the visible is a sign of the invisible. It is wrong to interpret the second member of this definition of faith as a simple parallel to the first; by such an interpretation, faith would relate to a hoped-for object, hence an object not yet existing and consequently not visible. In that context of thought the invisible would be future. Let us rather consider that the first part defines the faith of Abraham, focused on the future as the sphere of the fulfilment of the promise; faith is then the certainty of things hoped for; the second part, on the other hand, defines faith as experienced by Moses, whose faith pierced with its gaze the veil of the present, which offered itself to him as a sign of the presence of God. Faith is then the conviction that a presence which is not seen is none the less real.

The "descent" of God culminates, in the Mosaic perspective, in imposing as the essential theme of faith the idea of presence. It is the reality of this presence which is the support for faith, as it is also the occasion for some difficult but necessary processes of thought: how can it be that God is present? in what way is He present? how should man behave in face of this presence? how does this presence which at first is external to the believer become an internal presence for him? The Mosaic faith has, in view of its very structure, the duty of elucidating the problems relative to the mode of this presence and the means of participating in it.

This effort at elucidation will involve reflection in two directions, corresponding exactly to the very conditions of the presence of this God who has "come down", who is both transcendent and also incarnate in the flesh of this world.

On the one hand, the Mosaic faith will try to apprehend the divine transcendence in itself, in its metaphysical structure, so as to emphasize that no confusion is possible between God and the world. It will meditate on the supereminence of God in relation to the world, so as to assure a possibility of contact and yet to remove any reduction of the one to the other. It will seek to grasp the essence of this presence which is at the same time an absence, to understand how God assumes the real because He is the reality of realities. Mosaic reflection cannot help but issue in metaphysics.

Again, since the presence of God is revealed in an exterior way, the Mosaic type of faith is led to question itself about the possibility of a communication with the revealed God. It will meditate upon the part which revelation itself has allotted to the earthly things which it uses as media. It will discern the metaphysical dimension of these things which, like the burning bush, are consumed from within by an inner fire which does not, however, destroy their intrinsic earthly nature. Mosaic thought feels it to be incumbent on itself to elaborate a doctrine of the visible sign of the invisible presence.

In short, we have here the reality of a divine presence which is reached when man penetrates beyond the veil of things and words. This is tantamount to saying that the Mosaic faith finds its crown and culmination in the experience of participation in the divine presence, in a friendly dialogue with God enshrouded in the thick dark cloud, like Moses, who was in effect the first of the mystics. When the narrative of the Book of Exodus relates that Moses lived forty days and forty nights in communion with God on Mount Sinai, abstaining meanwhile from eating or drinking, and that on his descent the skin of his face shone (Ex. 34:28–30) we recognize without difficulty, in this stylized language, the ascetic discipline of the mystic and the external marks, the stigmata, which are the sign of the abnormal experience through which he has passed.

73

Chapter 5

A GLANCE AT THE HISTORICAL DESTINY OF THE
TWO TYPES OF SPIRITUALITY

ABRAHAM. . . . Moses. . . . Two figures, two aspects of Biblical revelation. But also two styles of piety, two types of spirituality, two universes, each with its own internal logic, its implications, its consequences.

Biblical faith, taken in its unity and integrity, incorporates these two universes and in the crucible of living experience unites them the one to the other, brings them into solidarity with each other, balances them and corrects them, the one by the other, holding them in a dialectic which is at times dramatic.

In the interpretation which the church makes of scripture throughout the course of centuries it becomes clear that there is the greatest difficulty in maintaining this dialectic as a living and efficacious force. Each of these two complementary aspects of revelation has its own inherent and characteristic logic, its mode of thinking, its range of emotions, its intellectual and affective affinities. All these factors give rise to as many difficulties felt by believers, involved in one of the two perspectives, when they try to remain open and accessible to the riches of spirituality proper to the other.

By the force of things and the weakness of men, this difficulty of maintaining a fruitful dialogue between the two spiritual heritages which Abraham and Moses bequeathed will culminate in a progressive hardening of the respective positions, in an ever more marked emphasis on the characteristics proper to each. Finally, the distinction will become an opposition, and it will be thought necessary, out of loyalty to the heritage received, to fulminate anathemas against the other side.

The drama of Christian fidelity to Biblical revelation is in

74

fact the drama implied in the coexistence of the two worlds. The ideal would have been to allow two different but complementary spiritualities to dwell together in unity in the church, and to accept the tension which could not fail to have resulted. In just such a way the two great figures Peter and Paul dwelt together and quarrelled with each other in the first church, the two sharply etched prototypes of these two ways of understanding faith in the God of Jesus Christ, the God of Abraham and Moses. Drama will arise from the fact that it will be found impossible to maintain the balance; the unilateral development of one of the two constitutive principles to the detriment of the other—by, as it were, a cancerous hypertrophy—will make the whole body sick.

For our present purposes, there can be no question of giving a complete account of this history. For about ten centuries, with varying fortunes, it was found possible to maintain the balance of the two spiritualities, the two theologies. During this period no decisive event supervened to compromise lastingly the contribution which each had the mission of furnishing to the common good of the one faith.

It must be recognized, however, that slowly divergent orientations were outlined, intellectual and affective predilections affirmed. Little by little, a real disparity between the eastern and western branches of Christendom emerged.

The causes of this are many, and they are difficult to analyse and assess. Temperaments and cultures, engendering each other and confirming each other by mutual interaction, played their part, while to this must be added in the reckoning the concurrence of political, sociological, and economic circumstances.

Indisputably, Graeco-Roman culture and the Latin spirit affirmed their influence in the west, imposing logical rigour, the ascendancy of the juridical spirit, and the concern for exact definition and solid organization. Oriental Christianity, on the contrary, became subject to the attraction of illumination and gnosis.

In fact, the schism which divided the great church as early as 1053 brought fully to light a divergence of interests and views which had for long been maturing. The dispute over the *Filioque* clause, at the moment when it took place, was perhaps no more than a discussion between theologians about the doctrine of the Trinity. In reality, the critical historian of today may assign to it a bearing and scope which the protagonists in the affair in all probability did not think of attributing to it. Even if the orientals are perhaps doing violence to the facts when they invoke the *Filioque* as a justification, the latter has none the less the value of a symbol, and on that score may be adduced in our present argument.

Eastern Christianity has always emphasized far more than Western Christianity the function and the action of the Holy Spirit. In this way it has endeavoured to affirm and safeguard the "overflowing" of the earthly by the heavenly; it has steadfastly refused to confound the event with the institution, the eschatological with the actual; it has wished to preserve for every mystery an open door to a beyond which should be its glorification. This tendency of its thought was manifested in the maintenance of the *epiklesis* in the eucharistic liturgy; the church must pray that the Holy Spirit should be outpoured on the gifts and the faithful. The Latin church, on the contrary, attributes to the priest the power of pronouncing *in persona Christi* efficacious words for the production of consecration. In that context the liberty and the living action of Christ are placed in the power of the historical institution; the Holy Spirit merges with this, which by definition He indwells.

This divergence in understanding of the mystery, which for oriental Christianity is reserved, heavenly, and of the world to come, and for western Christianity is institutionalized, earthly, and present, finds its reflection in the adoption by the westerns of a "realistic" type of thought; things are what they are, they are not open to a beyond which would be their future fulfilment; while the orientals persistently reject this "realism", which, they fear, could block the world and the church in sterile immobility. It is apparent that the quarrel over the *Filioque* is not unconnected with this diversity in the general perspectives characteristic of the two branches of Christianity; for by binding the Holy

Spirit to the Father, who in divinity is the dogmatic locus of unknowability—the divine person affirmed in its ultimate unfathomability—the Orient was safeguarding for the Holy Spirit a heterogeneity over against every historical manifestation. To affirm, on the contrary, with the west that the Holy Spirit proceeds from the Father *and* the Son is to bind the Holy Spirit to the historical act of revelation and to commit the Spirit to the concrete forms of the action of Christ in His church.

When the Eastern Orthodox Christian utters the prayer of *epiklesis* he asks God "to give us mysteriously the Christ through the Holy Spirit, to manifest the virtue of the incarnation, to send anew into the world the Son and the Holy Spirit".[1] The Western Catholic has no need of this deviation through the direct invocation of the Father in order that he may participate in the living presence of the Holy Spirit; he thinks that the church here below has at its disposal the virtue of the incarnation, since the Son has transmitted it to the priesthood. Hence we may with justice speak of the "basic eschatologism"[2] of Orthodox spirituality, or of an epikletic theology, that is, one which is penetrated with the idea of a fulfilment awaited in prayer. The tonality of this faith echoes that of Abraham. And if, looking in the other direction, we underline the Western Catholic tendency and temptation to crystallize and even to confine revelation within certain historical realities, certain ecclesiastical or conceptual institutions, within the dogmatically defined priesthood or dogmatic definitions in general, we notice the kinship of the central aim of this theology with the outlook of the Mosaic faith, which was here eventually pushed beyond its true limits.

The coexistence of the two divergent but complementary inspirations did not last. Tension led to rupture. The misfortune of division lastingly overshadowed the life of the Christian church through the lack of balance brought about in each of the complementary terms by its breaking off the dialogue with the other.

Theoretically one might have hoped that the protest

---

[1] S. Bulgakov, *Le Paraclet*, 1946, p. 372.

[2] P. Evdokimov, *L'Orthodoxie*, Neuchâtel-Paris, 1959, p. 9.

which was made five centuries later in the west would restore the compromised situation. When Luther rebelled against the Roman church it was indeed to remind men of the God of Abraham and of St. Paul, to remind them of the liberty of God over against human institutions, even over against His own gifts which never become an assured possession at the disposal of faith. Luther thundered against the Judaic interpretation of Moses, just as Paul had done before him. When he burnt the papal bull his gesture recalled that sharp conflict which led Paul to oppose Peter publicly, before all (Gal. 2:14), because the latter was "judaizing".

Unfortunately the difficult circumstances in which this reform of the church had to be made exceeded the strength of the men who undertook it. In the name of Abraham's faith, Luther reacted against the cancerous hypertrophy of Mosaism in the Roman church; but in opposing the evil which was making Christendom sick and unbalanced, he was led to make too exclusive a claim in favour of the Abrahamic spirituality. He alone cannot be held responsible for having set up a type of distortion contrary to the one he was denouncing and for having neglected the complementary factors inherent in the Mosaic faith. By far the greater responsibility in this situation lies at the door of the religious authority of the time. Luther was quite rightly fulfilling his mission as a prophet when he unilaterally emphasized the prophetic aspect of Biblical faith, the sovereignty and the freedom of God. It was indeed necessary that the trumpet should burst forth with no uncertain blast to overcome the tin-like jingling emitted by the religiosity of the day. It was not the aim of the reformer to establish a church, but to purify the Church; and no one today, not even the catholic theologian, would dispute that it needed such purification. The pope of the time might have given proof of his spiritual perspicacity by welcoming Luther's demands in favour of the Abrahamic current of inspiration, and by himself taking in hand the needed reform of the church. It was to him that Luther had appealed.

The enormous misfortune that resulted was that the reformation had to be made outside the framework of the official church of the time, and consequently in counter-action to it, so that by the very necessities of the situation it was driven to assume a sharply polemical character. The Lutheran claim in favour of the spirituality derived from Abraham was justified in the bosom of the church inasmuch as it was a prophetic message bearing its intrinsic authority within the total communion of the ecclesiastical body. But transported outside the duly constituted church, as soon as it became the basis of an autonomous ecclesiastical group it took on the character of an exclusive and unilateral claim, for the spirituality derived from Moses, contested on account of its Romanist perversions, could no longer serve as a complement to it.

The schism of Eastern Orthodoxy, which had taken place five centuries earlier, had already committed the church of Christ to the fatal necessity of no longer being able to react sanely to an effort of restoration such as that attempted by Luther. In the 16th century was it still possible even to understand the message of Luther? Had not the Western church already so sadly forgotten the very language of Abrahamic spirituality that it was incapable of perceiving the truth of Luther's protest? If theological positions had not been hardened by the unilateral development of Western Christendom subsequent to the schism of 1053 it might still have been possible to hear and to heed the voice of the Lutheran reformation. After five hundred years there would have been needed, in order to hear and assimilate it, men such as are rarely to be found even in the church of Christ.

Hence the reformation had to develop outside the bounds of the traditional church, combated by the latter, forced into a kind of competitive position, and constrained by the force of circumstances to adopt as the constitutive principle of its thought a truth which, to be sure, was originally and purely Biblical but which could not remain authentically Biblical except when conjugated, completed, enriched, and tempered by a complementary Biblical truth. The witness to truth borne by the churches of the reformation necessarily suffered from the polemical conditions in which those churches acquired form and extension.

It is right to note that Calvin brought to the Lutheran

reformation an important corrective, and a necessary complement. Calvin reacted against certain aspects of Luther's message which were too exclusively Abrahamic in character. The Mosaic faith finds an echo in Calvin, for instance in regard to "the external means or helps, which God uses to invite us to come to Jesus Christ His Son and to keep us in Him"—for so runs the title given by the author to the fourth book of the *Institutes*. It is easy and obvious to draw a comparison between the situation of Luther and that of Abraham, underlining the necessity of rupture, which made of both of them great initiators. The comparison could be pursued by drawing a parallel between Moses and Calvin, the heirs, the successors whose task it was to organize peoples and churches in the midst of difficult circumstances. One could point out the interest which Calvin showed in the church which he calls the mother of all the faithful, in those "external helps, by which", he says, "faith is engendered in us, grows in us, and advances from stage to stage"; one might note as significant that in introducing this subject Calvin refers precisely to Moses, declaring that the dispensation of the church "did not exist only under the law, but continues since the coming of Jesus Christ: witness St. Paul who declares that we are children of the new and heavenly Jerusalem" (Gal. 4:26). The law, for him, is not merely a matter of the ten commandments "but the form of religion, as God made it known by the hand of Moses".[1]

The correction which Calvin brought to the prophetic message of Luther was necessary, but did not prove itself sufficient. One might doubt whether, in view of the corrupt Mosaism of the Roman system, it would have been possible to adopt a better position. The fact remains that historic Calvinism failed to give to Christianity a renewed understanding of the spirituality derived from Moses. In the last resort the fault lies with those who, as disciples of Calvin, remained too rigorously faithful to the letter and perhaps indeed betrayed the deeper intention of their master. Let us add, however, in exculpation of them, that the fiercely hostile attitude of catholics, both theologians and politicians, towards the reformers inevitably induced the latter to stiffen

[1] *Inst.* II. 7. I.

their positions. On both sides stronger dogmatic barriers were erected in the desire to protect the faith from all contagion. Distances were widened. Anything in the nature of dialogue quickly became impossible. The strength of each system affirmed itself through the refutation of the opposing one.

In fact, the reform of the church had failed. In the first place, for the reason that those Christians who were convinced of the legitimacy of Luther's claim were constrained, in consequence of their rejection by Rome, to constitute a church outside the Church. That, however, was not the most serious defect. The true failure resides in the fact that Christians did not succeed in reconciling the two basic and complementary inspirations of the spiritualities stemming respectively from Abraham and Moses. The failure of the reformation was perhaps already sealed by the schism of 1053, which had been the cause of a unilateral development of Mosaic piety in the west. When Luther's protest in favour of the Abrahamic type of piety occurred it could hardly avoid the double misfortune of assuming a unilateral form because it had to confront a development which was itself unilateral, and of thus presenting itself in a way which was so much the more unacceptable and which drove the other side to a counter-offensive. The end result of the attempt at reform in the 16th century was to give a separate and divided existence to the two streams of inspiration, Abrahamic and Mosaic, which thus became isolated from each other in a sterile rivalry instead of coexisting in a mutually complementary way.

Chapter 6

PROTESTANTISM AND CATHOLICISM CONSIDERED AS HEIRS OF THE TWO TYPES OF SPIRITUALITY, ABRAHAMIC AND MOSAIC

THE rapid glance which we have just cast at the course of Christian history must now be completed by an examination of the concrete forms which the heritages of Abraham and Moses have assumed in the two great confessions, protestant and catholic. In fact, the attentive reader of the chapter devoted to the respective characteristics of these two types of spirituality will have noticed that the pattern of the spirituality stemming from Abraham already gives us a rudimentary definition of the spirit of protestantism, just as the pattern of the Mosaic heritage furnishes us with a clue to the understanding of catholicism. We must now try to carry this study a little further.

What constitutes the characteristic—and at the same time the temptation—of protestantism, flows from the very principle of Abrahamic spirituality. Man is addressed directly by the word of God, who intervenes, free and sovereign, at the very heart of the human being to sound in its depths His imperious call. Protestantism will always be suspicious of anything that threatens to become a substitute for this inner voice. God acts by means of a word, and this word, like every word, is addressed to personal being.[1] The relation of the believer to God will be essentially a personal dialogue. This word is an interior reality, bearing its evidence in itself; it is sealed in the heart by its own intrinsic

[1] In the argument which follows the reader should understand the expression "word of God" in its broadest sense, including at one and the same time the word which God speaks, Jesus Christ as the Word of God, and finally preaching, which, on the basis of Holy Scripture, proclaims the divine word in both these aspects.

virtue, or, what comes to the same thing, it is sealed by the Holy Spirit. When He speaks, God needs nothing and no one to make Himself understood.

This inner event arising from the word of God heard and received as such, when taken in its full seriousness with all its mystery and depth of meaning, removes from the horizon of faith and reflection any mediation borrowed from the realities of this world, from things or from men. Anything which cuts into the dialogue engaged by God with the believer—with the sole exception of Holy Scripture, since it is the organ of the Word of God—will be suspected of dimming its luminous clarity, or of perverting its essential nature.

On the one hand, protestantism will, in consequence, be extremely anxious to guard the "responsibility" of the believer, to see that he is given the possibility and the obligation to make a "response". No one can take the place of him whom God summons. To a certain extent even, no one other than he knows what God says to him, and no one can answer in his place or answer for him. Protestantism, ever fruitful in the generation of strong personalities, will bring to a climax of meaning such words as "conscience" and "responsibility".

On the other hand, since the word of God strikes to the very heart of a man's being, it is difficult to see what role can be assigned, in the life of faith, to those "external things" of which Luther spoke so severely. Faith distrusts the illusory support of these external media, of consecrated objects, ritual gestures, hallowed places, of that entire equipment of piety which, on the pretext of helping the believer, empties the divine call of the exigency and the weight which it carries for the person addressed. The dialogue springing from faith is direct and immediate. The protestant will always be inclined to denounce as materialistic or magical any insertion of divine grace into a reality of this world. He will repudiate anything which to him will appear as an undue stress on the physical, the material, aspect of things. He will reserve, one might say, as the exclusive mode and sphere of the divine action, the event of God's word. He will insist on the personal character of this word. He will prefer to consider it as an appeal, a call, a summons. He will be little or not at all interested in the conceptual content of this word. Truth for him will be mainly a principle of living, not a mode of knowledge. When God speaks, it is not to reveal an abstract and static truth, which one would be called upon to "believe", that is, to assent to. God speaks to proclaim the good news of what He has done and what He will do, so that the hearer may offer himself in his life and work in the obedient attitude of faith. This implies submission to the word, and consists in an expectation of the fulfilment of the promise declared by the word. We have here something dynamic and vital. The word is true not because it imposes its truth on the mind but because it quickens the soul of the one who receives it.

For protestantism, in consequence of this dominating category of the word, the relation of man to God is understood as a relation of person to person. Whether such a relation is good or bad means simply that there is dialogue or that the dialogue is interrupted. Sin is not a sullying stain, something which vitiates the being. It is a situation, and above all, a situation of rupture with God, an impiety. For this reason, protestantism regards sin in a radical way. Once the relation of dialogue with God is cut off, man continues indeed to be the man who he is; but the break which has supervened means that he has ceased to be the man whom God quickens and inspires. He is reduced to what he is, to live by his own resources and for his own interests, and this constitutes the radical sin. We might perhaps sum it up by saying that it is not his nature which is corrupted but his vocation which is destroyed. The word of God will not make of him the person he was called to be. This radical character of sin makes nonsense in a properly ontological perspective, that is to say, a static perspective. On the other hand, the idea of radical sin is easily understandable in the context of an Abrahamic anthropology, which places man in the perspective of the vocation laid upon him by the word of God and defines him in the light of a personal relationship to God.

Similarly, the restoration of the broken relationship will form the essence of the grace which removes sin and its consequences. Protestantism has emphasized the forensic character of the justification of the sinner; which means that it has understood justification as a change in the relation of man with God, in the situation of man before God. The sinner is justified inasmuch as the gratuitous favour of God establishes with him a new relationship, in which he can once more listen to the word of God and by that very fact receive the principle of life of which the rupture brought about by sin had deprived him. It is not the case that justification remains a purely external work or that God pronounces over the sinner false and fictitious words, declaring him to be righteous when in fact he is not. For the truth is that he is righteous from the moment when God proclaims him to be so, since in letting him know that he is proclaimed righteous, God restores the right relationship. The sinner is truly justified, if we define the righteous man as the one who is in a situation of dialogue with God, who is really reached and moved by the word of God. This justification determines sanctification, which is the characteristic work of the word received and assimilated in the heart of the believer. The word which proclaims justification (i.e. the restoration of the right relationship) fulfils the promise implied in this very proclamation.

The believer who sees things from this point of view could not consider that he is an agent in the process which restores his status in the eyes of God, any more than he is an agent in the work performed by the word which strikes at the heart of his being. Not only is forgiveness, and the absolving grace which restores the "righteousness" of the sinner (i.e. the situation of dialogue), the effect of God's operation alone, but also and to the same extent it is that sanctifying grace which works in his soul. God alone speaks in this dialogue; the believer can do no more than reply, that is, echo a word uttered by another. And in a sense we might say that this reply itself, because it is in its essence but an echo, is spoken within us by God Himself. This formula is not perhaps altogether rigorous and cannot be taken literally, but it well expresses the most basic conviction of the believer who is justified and sanctified by the word of God; the conviction, namely, that he is reached by an initiative and moved by the power of a love which has done for him and in him what he himself by his own resources would never have desired or been able to do. When he stresses the gratuitousness of the initiative and the sovereign freedom of the intervention, the protestant is not behaving as a religious masochist; he is expressing his joyous certitude and his heartfelt thankfulness at finding himself the object of so totally undeserved and free a favour, of a succour so truly efficacious. The doctrine of predestination is the culmination of this consciousness of assurance and thankfulness; a culmination in which we must not take too literally the concepts made use of, but in which we must seek the deeper meaning—a meaning imparted to it by a living faith and its own intrinsic demands. This doctrine is a projection, on the plane of temporal thought, of the certainty that salvation is entirely the work of God, and of God alone.

For all these reasons, protestant piety will be essentially interior and personal. It will remain centred in this dialogue of person with person, which God initiated in calling Abraham, the prophets, the apostles, and finally in sending Him who is the Word made flesh. To listen to the word of God—that is the centre of worship, private as well as public. The function of Holy Scripture as the locus of the word is consequently greatly increased in importance. Protestantism can apply to scripture what God said to Moses regarding the ark: "it is there that I will meet with you" (Ex. 25:22; a decisive difference should, however, be noted, namely, that the "place" of meeting is a book, that is to say, a word, and that the meeting consists in a dialogue).

It is understandable that protestantism should be greatly concerned to assure itself that the encounter, the dialogue, takes place in the best conditions. Since God speaks, man must listen, and listen to Him alone. Human words, the glosses which man adds to the word of God, the amassing of traditions and accretions, are suspected of threatening the wholeness and purity of this word. The principle of "free examination" is acknowledged to be indispensable, because the believer must be free to reject any other "word" in order that he may offer himself fully to the reading and understanding of the word of God. This "free examination" implies a basic accessibility of the believer when confronted by the scriptures which he is examining. Faith must make of scripture a study and a meditation which will be free from all prejudice, all bias, all human oversight, so that the authority of the word of God may find full scope and exercise and that this word may alone exercise such ultimate authority.

Protestantism has sometimes been characterized by reference to its concern for purity. It is a fact that the logic of the doctrine of the God who speaks—which is central for protestantism—leads to the elimination of all ancillaries which might impair the directness of God's intervention through His word. Purity is here an internal necessity. If God speaks, nothing else can be taken into consideration except His word, i.e. His message in its immediacy. This involves firstly a radical devaluation of all the material of piety with which the religious man is wont spontaneously to surround himself; secondly, the no less radical elimination of any activity or causality which might enter into competition with that of God: God alone speaks. It is in the very nature of protestantism to repudiate the pairs which catholicism tends to create: Bible *and* tradition, word *and* sacrament, faith *and* works, Jesus Christ *and* the Virgin Mary, etc. Because the word of God is an inner event, no external reality can either contain it or guarantee it; and because this word is that of God, nothing can intervene to better it or to complete it; it has its necessary and sufficient efficacy in itself; it can enter into composition with nothing whatsoever. To claim to add to it, is to fail to recognize its supernatural essence, and to compromise its sovereign virtue and authority. This concern for purity manifests in the protestant world not an iconoclastic blindness, but the obedience of a faith which aspires to nothing other than its own proper object.

The attitude of protestantism towards the sacraments and doctrinal formulations bears the mark of this same concern. It is true that sacraments and dogmas continue to play their part in the life of protestantism. But they have not a very secure place in its thought, and they are not the object of an equal fervour. External things can only appear suspect in comparison with that event which goes on in the secret place of the soul and which is its dialogue with God. How should their natural unwieldiness and materiality be adjusted to the essentially spiritual character of such an event? The same applies to words, which seem very inapt to grasp the contours of a faith that is lived. The very idea of a *ne varietur* definition of the truth offends protestant sensibility because it compels one to reduce the mystery of faith to the dimensions of human language. It is true, of course, that Biblical language is also a human language, and that the word of God in the Bible is found in the form of a word of man, but there is postulated for this language a privilege of inspiration which protestant theology and preaching alike will always be inclined to stress more than is done among catholics. By extreme contrast with the infallible definition of dogma which is congenial to the Roman outlook, we shall note the refusal of certain protestants to define the faith otherwise than by quoting Biblical texts.

In a more general sense, the fact that the protestant's attention is focused on the event of the word of God leads him to doubt the value of human language altogether; in particular, he questions the possibility of crystallizing the essence of the inner event of faith in the form of propositions rationally constructed. Nominalism is not, for protestant thought, a position theoretically reached in reaction to the conceptualist objectivism which has for long dominated and fashioned Christian philosophy. In reality, protestantism is not nominalist in the exact sense of the term; it simply wishes to respect the zone of mystery with which faith must be surrounded so long as that human condition lasts of which the apostle Paul wrote that its knowledge is more or less obscure (1 Cor. 13:9–12).

In the same circle of ideas, it is equally interesting and useful to notice the observation, often made in a hostile sense, that protestantism is fideism. In such a context the critic understands by fideism the superiority assigned to the affective over the intellectual element in the life of faith, the favour and prestige enjoyed by emotion and intuition to the disadvantage of reason. The fact is indisputable; its significance, on the other hand, will become apparent only if we understand it in the light of the whole conception of God's word. It is not a question of reducing the divine object to the dimensions of the subject, as is thought by those who wish to entrust to reason the task of safeguarding the objectivity of the faith through rational formulation. We must see in this, rather, the consequence of the primacy accorded to the word of God heard, assimilated, and lived out by the believer. To the extent to which the words *experience* and *existence* can be purged of the parasitic meanings which have been attached to them on account of those philosophical or theological schools which have monopolized their use, we shall say that fideism is connected with the essentially experiential character of faith, which concerns always the believer at the deepest core of his existence.

It would not be difficult to show that the use of Holy Scripture in protestantism is likewise determined, in its fundamental approach, by the same general presuppositions. The protestant reads scripture as the word of God, that is, he approaches it as one enters into a dialogue; he knows himself to be challenged, scripture faces him with a question; it calls into question his whole life; in reading it, he knows himself to be summoned and called to account by God, he knows he is obliged to respond. Certainly scripture contains historical and doctrinal truths; in principle, the protestant cannot be indifferent to this, for it is through the facts reported and the doctrines expounded that God makes His voice to be heard. Nevertheless, this element of objective, historical, or doctrinal truth is only the outward husk, the channel, the "flesh"—in a word—of a message which transcends it absolutely. The important and essential does not lie on the plane of such truth, which is not directly relevant to the existence of the human being in faith. This consideration explains the fact that the protestant critic can show himself to be so free in his judgments concerning historicity, the fact that his laboratory work seems to ruin a book on which his faith is nourished in his oratory. No one would doubt that there are difficulties in this apparent dichotomy which marks the critical protestant interpretation of scripture. The important point which concerns us here is merely to indicate the source of it, so as to facilitate its understanding.

Focused on the inner life, distrustful with regard to "external things", protestant spirituality adheres to the individual and the invisible. The conjunction of these two preferences makes protestantism little appreciative of the values of church life. The protestant is inclined to apply to ecclesiological matters the text in which the apostle Paul compares the old covenant to the earthly Jerusalem and the new to the heavenly Jerusalem. The protestant's predilection is for the heavenly Jerusalem. The church is a reality so inward and so secret that it cannot but be invisible; God alone knows who properly belongs to it. The people of God, as a people, is certainly a visible and earthly reality; but the life that it now lives in the flesh, the protestant again would say with St. Paul, it lives by faith in the Son of God; as people *of God*, it exists only by virtue of faith. God does not establish its foundations in this world; nothing can guarantee its quality; it is the church only as it turns on the axis of faith. That is why for the protestant the church cannot be an institution, an objective concrete reality which abides in itself. It appears rather, *hic et nunc*, in the very act which makes it emerge as a reality of faith, when believers assemble to heed in faith the word of God, or when they confess their faith before the world.

Luther set the tone of protestant tendencies in ecclesiology when he discontinued the use of the word *church*. He chose to recognize only the word *Gemeinde*, that is, the community of believers, the group of *viatores*, of pilgrims who pass through this world with their eyes fixed on the distant horizon which has been disclosed to their faith by the promise implied in God's word. There can be no question of any establishment in this world which would denote a yielding to the temptation to anticipate the last times, the ultimate aeon. In order to remain dependent on the promise and the promise alone, the Christian must resist the temptation to set up in the present age an organized institution in which the human will would have, at its free disposal and exercise, that which can depend only on the sovereign liberty of God.

We notice here one of the salient features of protestant spirituality, namely, its eschatological note. The fact of relying only on the word which God utters, on the promise which that word makes known, and on its secret effects in the heart, turns faith aside from whatever is not that word itself, that promise, that foreshadowed grace in which the soul participates only in so far as it waits for it. The gift cannot be substituted for the promise. If faith begins to contemplate the grace granted, then it turns in upon itself and turns away from the promise and Him who has made it. Like Abraham offering in sacrifice the son who was none the less the gift of the promise, protestant spirituality refuses to fasten its attention on the work already accomplished by grace. The promise is truly a promise; it remains a promise in spite of that part of it which might already have been realized. The protestant does not doubt that God sanctifies the believer and the church; but he cannot allow his thought to linger over this aspect of the divine intervention in human history lest it should become fettered to it. Salvation is always beyond and above whatever he has seized and apprehended of it, beyond all that has been attained; it lies in a future which faith characteristically makes present for the believer who awaits it trustfully. Protestant prayer will have the nature of intercession rather than adoration, for the same reason as protestant preaching will consist in an appeal rather than instruction. Obedience consists not in enjoying to the full what one is or what one has, but in aspiring ever beyond, in an attitude of unceasing expectation. Faith cannot canalize spiritual values, whether in a life, an institution, or a formula. What one awaits from the word of God always exceeds what human words can express. The Christian must ask and seek, rather than examine himself to see whether he has received the gift; he must praise God for the promise rather than concentrate his attention on a completed fulfilment.

Protestantism could not fail to give special favour to the doctrine of the Holy Spirit, for it is this doctrine which accounts for the different structural elements of protestant piety and thought and which secures their unity. Historically, it is clear that the reformation was a "spiritual" movement and that the greatest danger it incurred, and which always faces protestant piety, is the danger of succumbing

91

to the errors engendered by the "enthusiasm" of those who maintain that they enjoy the special guidance and inspiration of the Spirit. Conversely, it cannot be doubted that the reaction against the "enthusiasts" of all ages has favoured the catholic tendency at the heart of Christian thought.

Protestantism has always fostered a certain sympathy towards those who, whether true prophets or, as it turned out, false prophets, have rightly or wrongly made clear the liberty of God over against all human institutions, the dynamism of grace running counter to the sclerotic tendency of rightly thinking conformism. The protestant would like to believe that he has the monopoly of the prophetic spirit. There is much illusion in this claim, if not pride; nevertheless, protestant spirituality, by favouring the direct relation of the soul with God, creates a situation propitious for the manifestation of the liberty of God, impinging upon man directly through the agency of the Holy Spirit.

If protestantism is simple, catholicism is complex. The simplicity of protestantism is for it a kind of internal necessity; the simpler it is, the more it conforms to its basic principle, for the intervention of the word of God fundamentally precludes any idea of composition or synthesis. "Purity", sobriety, austerity have become for protestantism almost the essential marks of authenticity.

Catholicism is complex, and equally its complexity stems from its fundamental principle. Again, one can say of it that the more complex it is, the more it conforms to its own essential nature. It obeys a logic of integration, just as protestantism obeys a logic of purgation and elimination. It is comprehensive and synthetic, whereas protestantism is exclusive and analytic.

The reason for this contrast became apparent from the very origins of the Mosaic faith. With Moses, one might say, the revelation made to Abraham "came down" from heaven to earth; it entered into the continuity of history, it became interwoven with the life of the world, assuming concrete forms. Absolute in its essence, which of course it remains, it now becomes relative in its manifestations, it becomes contingent, mixed, disputable. Whereas the word of God committed Abraham to a way which involved him in a decisive break, depriving him of all "worldly" support, and compelling him to walk ahead as seeing nothing, his attention absorbed by the eschatological promise, the word of God disclosed itself to Moses in the shape of sensuously apprehensible phenomena, in visible and audible signs, and to that extent it entered into composition with and was compromised by that which was not authentically itself. The revelation granted to Moses inaugurated a delicate dialectic of nature and grace.

Historic catholicism develops according to the inner rhythm imposed on it by this dialectic. It will be at one and the same time preoccupied by the concern to do full justice to all that is implied by this insertion of the word of God in the "flesh" of this world, and careful also not to confound this same word with its concrete, visible, and historical instruments. The tension which results from this double concern will lead it to accentuate the characteristics proper to each of the terms brought together, so as to avoid their mutual absorption. For this reason, catholicism always tends to give the self-contradictory appearance of a spirituality which is indissolubly linked to the "physical", the natural, and which at the same time is anxious to affirm the "metaphysical", the *super*-natural.

The two axes about which catholic spirituality revolves are thus placed in position. On the one hand, historical embodiment; on the other, the stress laid on transcendence. On the one side, it will be emphasized that the church is a perfect society; on the other, the sense of divine mystery will be fostered and developed.

The catholic doctrine of the church throws into strong relief the Mosaic principle of the "descent" of God. If, in an act of condescension, God has come down, it is assuredly not to leave here below no more than the memory of His passage. The incarnation is the decisive event for faith. In the idea that the God who has descended among us has withdrawn and that we now find ourselves in the *status quo ante*, there is something not only shocking for faith but also incomprehensible for logic. The incarnation calls into being the church, which is in a sense a prolongation of the

93

incarnation, the incarnation made present and sensible throughout the course of historic time. It is impossible to over-emphasize the importance of this, and we must consider with religious attention the motives, the conditions, and the consequences of the incarnation.

The God of Abraham who speaks to Moses reveals Himself to the latter principally as the compassionate God. Inheriting as it does the faith of Moses, catholic spirituality emphasizes the theme of divine pity by placing the whole life of the believer under the sign of the maternal solicitude of the church. The church is the product of the compassionate will of the God who has come down from His heaven because He has seen the wretchedness of His people. The fundamental reason for the existence of the institution lies in the redemptive purpose of God, in the need to adapt His plan of love to the concrete conditions of human existence, so that He may give to the movement of His love the forms and the means which will secure for it the necessary efficacy for the attainment of its end. God is the father of believers; the church is their mother. The believer knows that he is taken in charge by the preventive grace and mercy of God who does not cease to seek an approach to him, to "descend" through the ministry of the church.

Such is the divine motive for the institution of the church. It is understandable that catholic piety clings to the church as to the absolute condition of its existence, a postulate of faith. Incarnation and church cannot be dissociated from each other. In passing let us note that the importance which, from the start, is assigned to the incarnation as the theological source of the doctrine of the church compels the catholic to insist, in a quite special way, on the concrete— let us say even maternal—character of the incarnation. The "descent" of God becomes a problem if we wish to give an account of it, or at least if we wish to speak of it in a way which guarantees the full "carnal" reality of this incarnation. Hence we must not be surprised at the interest, both religious and speculative, which catholic thought and piety show in the Virgin Mary, the locus of the incarnation. The doctrine elaborated around the figure of the Virgin Mary has been interpreted as a form taken by the pretentiousness of human nature, which thus claims to co-operate with redemptive grace. This doctrine—setting aside, of course, its deplorable corruptions—assumes quite a different aspect if it is seen in connection with the problematics of the incarnation. The decisive importance assigned to the "descent" of God among men in the Person of His Son Jesus Christ urges the catholic thinker to consider the conditions in which this intervention took place. In exalting the mother of Jesus, catholic spirituality desires to express the reality of the incarnation while at the same time under-lining the mystery which constitutes its essence. It is seeking to secure its own foundations.[1]

Hence we must not consider this prominence given to the church (and to the Virgin Mary) apart from the doctrine of the incarnation. The will to power shown by certain princes of the church has given rise to the belief that the origin and the end of the institution was to assure scope for the exercise of temporal power. Many vicissitudes in the history of the church, on the level of those contingencies which no human society can escape, have confirmed this impression. On the other hand, the perversions which Marian piety has suffered to the point of degenerating into indisputable abuses, have justified the apprehensions of the inheritors of the faith of Abraham, who have found in the cult no sufficient basis either in scripture or in the doctrine of the word of God.

This way of approaching from the outside the doctrine of the church and Mariology (which is only a special expression of the former) does not enable one to understand what is really at issue. In order to enter into the catholic perspective, we must have recourse to the category of *presence* which flows from the idea of incarnation. God has made Himself present to man; He has "come down" into the very heart of this world. The faith of Moses is con-stituted by the revelation of this compassionate divine condescension; and the catholic faith has drawn out all the

---

[1] Of course, secondary motives have contributed to the development of Mariology, notably the desire to compensate, by pointing to the humanity of Mary, the excessive emphasis on the divinity of her Son. Nor are psychological motives negligible.

consequences of this revelation which was decisively confirmed by Jesus Christ. From the point of view of the
catholic faith, protestantism has every appearance of having
remained at the stage of John the Baptist, and of having
forgotten that the Son of God has stooped to dwell among
us. In other words again, it seems to ignore the fact that
the revelation granted to Abraham finds its completion
and necessary complement in the revelation granted to
Moses.

Catholic spirituality assigns to the notion of presence the
same part as protestant spirituality assigns to the notion
of the word. It is impossible to understand how the elements
of catholicism cohere unless we take into account this basic
notion. Similarly, there is a parallel between the ideas of
word and approach; the word becomes a reality when
dialogue is engaged; the presence becomes a reality when it
draws near or when man draws near to it. Dialogue tends
to create a spiritual communion; presence permits rather a
communication of itself. In the idea of presence there is
always a spatial connotation, a sort of localization. The
latter expression goes too far, if it encloses the presence in
question within a defined space and confuses it with the
matter which fills that space. Sometimes the term quasi-
localization is used to indicate this presence, which is in a
place but is not that place itself.

The church is pre-eminently the locus of this presence, a
locus which is both visible and invisible, concrete and ideal,
the sphere of the presence and of the self-communication of
God. The church is an area defined and determined by a
divine presence, the sacral space where God may be ap-
proached. It is the means by which He exercises His pitying
and redemptive action. In the idea of the church cohere
the spatial and the personal elements implied by the
presence of God; presence of a person, presence in some
place. In short, as St. Paul says, the church is the "Body of
Christ"—the expression gathering its full significance from
the incarnation, to which it must be referred.

Catholic piety has an acute sense of this divine presence.
It may be considered that here faith finds its crown in the
certainty that God approaches man through the media of

the whole concrete reality of the church (and in particular through the sacraments), a reality which accompanies the word proclaimed by the church just as the concrete presence and the actions of Jesus Christ accompanied His preaching.

Hence for catholic ecclesiology there is an inescapable necessity for the visibility of the church. The idea that the church could be invisible is as self-contradictory as the idea of an incarnation which might not be fleshly. It is not that the catholic confuses what is seen of the church with its essence. The sign is not the same thing as the thing signified. The dialectic of nature and supernature finds here one of its many fields of application, and it is diversified according as to whether the church, the sacramental system, or the priesthood is in question.

The church is holy, but the person of its servants and their actions are not necessarily so in consequence. Function is distinct from the one who exercises it; the organ is placed in the service of a function which surpasses it. There may be some difficulty in understanding the "mystery" of a union which causes the spouse to share in the sanctity of the bridegroom because they are one "flesh", without authorizing the spouse to become fully identified with the bridegroom, still less to take his place. This "mystery" has been conjured up by St. Paul in the Letter to the Ephesians. The believer must understand that there is union without confusion and distinction without separation.

It is the same with regard to the sacramental system. This may likewise be envisaged, from the standpoint of the incarnation, as the manifestation of that "descent" of God who approaches man in a quasi-local way, who uses, to intimate His presence, certain "efficacious signs", certain visible and sensuous means calculated to "proclaim" and to accomplish through concrete actions what His word "proclaims" and accomplishes by means of human words. It is evident that catholic spirituality will tend to emphasize the importance of the sacramental sign because it understands the latter in its integral and essential relation to the incarnation. Before denouncing the exaggerations to which the practice and theology of the sacraments have given rise in catholicism, it is wise and right to attempt to grasp

97

the basic intentions underlying the system. The reader will recall that Mosaic piety had understood the revelation of the "descent" of God to be expressed in a kind of sacralization of time and space, implying that God was setting apart certain places and certain moments, which, in His pity, He established as the sphere of encounter offered to those who, seeking His presence, wished to draw near to Him.

Similarly with regard to sacred persons. The catholic doctrine of the priesthood is integrated within the whole perspective opened up by the incarnation; it flows from the certainty of the "descent" of God into the concrete, the historical, and finally the human. Moses already was the mediator who climbed the mountain to confront the terrible presence of God and who brought back from his encounter with God the words which God addressed to His people. God speaks, but His pity has willed to make His word more accessible, to adapt it to the conditions of those who were to receive it. The descent of the *Verbum Dei* into human flesh is the final term of this movement of divine condescension. It is a culmination which is sufficient and final because the Christ willed it to continue in the person of His apostles. The Christ was not able to render the presence of God which He incarnated effective and actual for all men; He made of His apostles His mouth for preaching, His hands for healing, His feet for travelling over the countryside of Judea. From that moment He has not ceased to animate with His spirit and His breath the "body" which He then constituted, that He might make His presence near and effectual, through the specialized members of His body, to every man, in every place, and at all times.

Among all the earthly objects which God assumes when His revelation finds an outlet in the sphere of the concrete, none is more important than the human object which He makes His organ of self-communication. Catholic spirituality emphasizes the dignity of the priesthood, inasmuch as it draws our attention to the compassionate initiatives of the God who condescends to adapt His redemptive action to the condition of those whom he wishes to save. The attitude of catholics towards the hierarchy, whether it be a question of the relations of the layman with the priest or of the relations of the priest with his superiors, is not to be explained as an attitude of servility or as something savouring of religious masochism. The catholic soul is bound, as to the fundamental condition of its faith, to the fact that God has "come down", embodying His intervention in precise circumstances; hence, for the catholic, to acknowledge his distance as regards the forms chosen by God for the purpose of making His presence real to His people, is to acknowledge his distance from God.

Priesthood and sacrament are indissolubly linked, as in the ministry of Christ His words and His deeds are linked, as in His person are the *Logos* and the *Sarx*. It is the word which creates the sacraments, and the sacraments fulfil what the word proclaims. A priesthood deprived of the concrete acts of the sacraments would remain, as it were, a word poised between heaven and earth, a disembodied preaching. Sacraments detached from the word would degenerate into magic ritualism, purely immanent.

It may be said that catholic spirituality finds its living centre in the eucharist, because there the presence of God is manifested in the most formal way. Eucharistic piety and theology crown the speculative and religious edifice of catholicism, precisely to the extent that this sacrament decisively confirms for the faith of believers the truth that God has effectually rendered Himself present to this world. All the more or less satisfactory or arbitrary explanations by which attempts have been made to account for the presence of God in the eucharistic sacrament have in reality hardly more relevance for its appreciation than, for the thirsty in need of water, has the learned explanation summed up in the formula H_2O. It is not in the discussion of these explanations that we can understand the significance that catholic piety finds in the eucharistic sacrament as the supreme means by which the spiritual thirst of the soul is quenched.

To unite without confusion, to distinguish without separation; nothing further can be said. Critical principles, these, which are doubtless vague but which one cannot clearly define in the circumstances any more than one can clarify the mystery of the burning bush, the enigmatic symbol of a presence which is not confounded with the thing that signifies it and which cannot be known except by means of that thing. God is there, but He is not present in virtue of the material reality which is apprehended by the senses. His presence consumes the object from within, and yet is not confused with that object; His presence negates it like the fire which reduces to ashes, but at the same time does not destroy it, since the presence makes use of it for the purpose of self-manifestation. Eucharistic realism is not materialism; it is the affirmation of a presence which is mysterious, ineffable, adorable.[1]

It thus becomes apparent that catholic spirituality which is focused on the idea of presence is inescapably orientated towards metaphysical reflection. It feels obliged to investigate the relations between the divine reality present in the objects of this world and those objects themselves, so as to define, as best the human mind may and in accordance with its requirements, how these two factors become united without confusion and are distinct without separation. Hence the catholic thinker must ask questions such as are familiar to those whose business it is to pierce beyond appearances in order to reach the real essence of reality, the substance behind the forms; it becomes essential to speak of ontology.

As, furthermore, the very "descent" of God into the heart of the realities of this world implies the possibility of such relations, the thinker must admit that, between God and the world, there is not an impassable gulf, an absolute metaphysical heterogeneity. This is why catholic thought, in order to clarify such relations, is fond of using the idea of analogy. The idea of analogy enables us to elucidate and understand complex relations between realities linked by bonds which unite them without confusing them, distinguish them without separating them.

Driven to philosophical reflection in order to search into the abstract problems of ontology and analogy, catholic

---

[1] For a few details on these points, cf. Franz J. Leenhardt, *"Ceci est mon corps", Explication de ces paroles de Jésus-Christ,* Neuchâtel 1955 (Eng. trans. in *Essays on the Lord's Supper,* Lutterworth Press, London; John Knox Press, U.S.A., 1958); or again: "La présence eucharistique", in *Irenikon,* XXXIII, 1960, pp. 146–72.

thought at the same time will be inclined to take a very positive view of concrete reality, to the extent that the divine presence, mysterious but assured, imparts to the latter a new and positive meaning. In fact, the divine presence calls upon it to play the part of an instrument for the expression of the supernatural, assigning to it the role of a secondary cause associated with the sole decisive and efficacious primary cause, namely, divine grace. The presence of God in the world can neither eliminate nor merge itself with natural causality, which it uses. Were it to eliminate natural causality, it would eliminate the world instead of being present to the world; were it to become merged with nature, it would eliminate itself. It is still the same dialectic, which explains why the idea of secondary causation has imposed itself on catholic thought as an instrument of reflection as necessary as it is convenient.

Catholic spirituality will apprehend the grace of God in the light of its faith in the presence of God, and will understand it as a communication of this presence. In the framework of a theology of the word of God, grace is, in the last analysis, that word itself; it is the resumption of the dialogue, the restoration of the personal relationship. For protestantism, grace carries a juridical resonance: God is gracious, He turns to the soul in mercy, addressing it anew with His life-giving word. But in the framework of a theology of the presence of God, grace is, in the last resort, that presence itself, that presence communicated and shared. For catholicism, the word grace carries an ontological resonance: God gives His grace, and for that purpose the sacraments were instituted, for they "contain" and "confer" grace itself,[1] thus assuring a kind of immediate contact between the believer and God who has come down to seek him.

Thus, from this point of view, the state of the believer will be characterized by his appropriation of what the sacraments have brought him, by that gift which is added to nature. The believer is enabled to share in the supernatural divine life, one might almost say that he is divinized—to express emphatically this idea of participation in the divine presence

[1] *Continere gratiam, gratiam ipsam conferre.* Denz., 849.

—just as for Moses the ground on which God manifested Himself and the altar on which He resided were sacred.

In this connection, we might notice another contrast which we have already observed as having been brought out by the bipartite definition of faith given at the beginning of chapter 11 of the Letter to the Hebrews. In the framework of a theology of the word of God, it is the category of the promise which is the dominant feature: the word is essentially a promise because it is an appeal, it prescribes a vocation, it opens up the horizons of the future which it creates; faith has an eschatological tonality; it rejects the various forms of installation in this world; it is a firm assurance of things hoped for. But within the framework of a theology of the presence of God, it is the category of the gift which is uppermost: the divine presence is the real, enriched and enhanced by the mystery of God already "present", actual, shared; faith possesses what it already beholds through the interposed signs; it seizes in the visible the "monstration" of that which is not seen. Thus catholic spirituality, without confusing the eternal and the temporal, draws them together in a kindly bond of union, so as to preserve to the compassionate movement of God's love its incarnational character. For this reason it will adhere to the actual and given forms of the divine presence, to its concrete manifestations, especially as they are to be found in the manifold aspects of the ecclesiastical institution. For this faith, the invisible furnishes itself with signs and shows itself to the believer. In its view "external things" are not simply external; they have a depth which is fathomed and sounded by the vision of a faith which sees what is invisible.

Thus we may understand the part played by visual representations in catholic piety. To say that protestantism is a religion of hearing and catholicism a religion of seeing is not without its truth. Catholic spirituality is led to cultivate that power and depth of vision which seeks meaning in the signs offered to the sight, even where protestant feeling is tempted merely to denounce formalism if not idolatry. Visible media are intended to stimulate a faith which sees what is invisible.

The dialectic of the visible and invisible, of the natural

and the supernatural, is manifested in the full tension of its antitheses by the very keen awareness of divine transcendence which is a mark of catholic spirituality. If it is only a detail, it is none the less a significant detail that the catholic believer speaks to God with greater reverence than does the protestant. Protestant prayer is more familiar, more direct, more spontaneous; it makes its requests in the second person. Catholic prayer is more liturgical; the personal element is less apparent in it; adoration and contemplation occupy a far greater place. It normally likes to use intermediaries, which help the soul to approach God and to overcome obstacles which would hinder the granting of prayer; such intermediaries are the intercession of the saints, the intercession of the church, and, above all, the intercession of the mediatrix of all graces, the Blessed Virgin Mary. One has indeed the impression that God is a splendid monarch and a severe judge, and that even the intercession of His Son is not sufficient to reassure the believer. Such intermediaries remind us of the part played by Moses when he intervened between the rebellious people and his angry God: "Forgive now their sin; if not, blot me out of Thy book which Thou hast written" (Ex. 32:32). In this situation Moses throws the whole weight of his mediatorial personality into the gulf between God and the people, his intercession is truly sacerdotal; it is his function which is jeopardized by the anger of God which threatens the people with ruin, and with that function the whole structure of revelation is threatened. Let us compare this intercession with that of Abraham praying for Sodom, and its essential character will stand out clearly. Abraham is very *protestant*, in his way of discussing the matter point by point with God as though on equal terms; he has all the appearance of wishing to instruct God on the duties attaching to His position. Yet he does not himself intervene; he does indeed intercede, but he is not a mediator. It is clear that absolutely anyone could pray to God as he does, whereas the person of Moses is not thus interchangeable.

The very keen consciousness of divine transcendence which we note in catholic spirituality has given scope to the development of a mysticism which has its own peculiar characteristics. Without wishing to give to these words too rigorous a bearing, we might say that Christian mysticism presents itself to our attention in two aspects. Now, the experience of communion with God is apprehended as the coming of God into the soul; now, it is understood as the exodus of the soul and its flight towards God. In the first case we have a mysticism governed by a movement of descent; it has a more personal character, and the person of Christ plays a determinative part in it; the soul knows itself to be indwelt by the presence which it has welcomed. In the mysticism of exodus, the soul aspires to be released from its bondage in order to ascend towards God; here an upward movement is predominant; by the practice of an ascetic discipline intended to free it from its servile condition the soul wills to reach a metaphysical sphere which is external to it. The descending type of mysticism leads to contemplation and the imitation of Christ; the ascending type leads to transforming knowledge and union. The former is an open mysticism, which permits an unceasing expectation of an increase of grace. The latter is a mysticism which is closed, confined within itself, in the sense that it fully attains the object of its striving when the soul gains access to that object; rare as are those moments, they are perfect in themselves; there lies nothing beyond; they cannot advance and develop, they can only be repeated.

Catholic spirituality is versed in both types of mysticism. It seems, however, to entertain a secret preference for the mysticism of ascent. Protestant spirituality is not unaware of the mysticism which depends on the descent of the divine, but it fosters an undoubted suspicion of the mysticism of exodus. A comparison of the mysticism of ascent with the spirituality of Moses is easy and near at hand; it resides in both words and things. The symbolism of the mountain climbed by Moses signifies the rupture of the bonds which hold the soul imprisoned. The ascetic discipline of purification is evoked by the forty days which Moses passed on the mountain without eating or drinking. By the annihilation of the natural powers of the soul, Moses encounters God in the "dark night", represented by the thick cloud in which God is concealed. After this encounter the face of Moses shines, radiating the glory of God. The God of the mysticism which involves the exodus of the soul resembles in many lineaments the God of Moses, and it is doubtless not accidental that mystical terminology has borrowed so much from the Old Testament.[1] The soul goes forth to the meeting with Him who resides in some sphere. "In a dark night ... I went forth"; thus begins the well-known poem of St. John of the Cross. The first strophe of his *Spiritual Canticle* likewise suggests the darkness and the distance of the spot in which the Well-Beloved dwells: "Where hast Thou hidden Thyself ... ? I went out after Thee crying and Thou hadst already departed." Such formulae are not simply literary; they bring vividly before us the deep basic structure of this mysticism, in which the soul is transported outside its normal habitation. How catholic mystical theology has systematized this ascent of the soul towards God is well known.

Catholicism and protestantism have harvested the heritages of Moses and Abraham respectively. They manifest two types of spirituality, two types of life and faith, likewise two modalities of theological reflection, two theological "mentalities".

The faith of Abraham is that proper to first beginnings and to ever fresh beginnings; the faith of Moses is concerned, above all, for continuity. The former is open to the future and richly pregnant with potentialities which the latter realizes, stabilizes, and builds into a coherent whole. The former may favour improvisation and anarchy, the latter is threatened by sclerosis and secularization. With the Mosaic spirituality, the liberty proper to the Abrahamic spirituality becomes a choice, the act becomes being.[2] Abraham's faith awaits from God what He is going to do, it thinks of God under the category of action; God is supremely the agent, He is active; God is "He who comes". The Mosaic faith contemplates what God has done; it thinks of God under the category of being; God is "He who is".

[1] Cf. the Life of Moses by Gregory of Nyssa, Carmel, the Song of Songs.

[2] The terms *act* and *being* are not used here with reference to any particular metaphysical system.

105

Protestantism and catholicism have always marked their preferences according to these general lines of orientation, both in theology and philosophy. Protestant dogmatics is inspired by a more personal and a more dynamic idea of God and His work; catholic dogmatics is inspired by a more metaphysical and static idea. In the former case it is existence, will, and freedom which are uppermost; in the latter case it is a question of essence, knowledge, and nature.

Chapter 7

CONCLUSIONS

IN fact, neither catholicism nor protestantism quite corresponds in practice to the picture which we have just painted of them. The observer would have to be singularly blind not to see the numerous and often very serious distortions which their basic principles have suffered in the course of historical developments.

Catholics will object—and they will be right in view of certain facts—that protestantism is *also* and in consequence unbridled individualism, that it makes for divisiveness in the church, that it promotes a wildly eccentric reading of the Bible, that it favours an absence of authority and a doctrinal and moral anarchy, that it culminates in a fideism which dissolves dogma, a nominalism which evacuates thought, etc. What is the use of going on? All the ills of the modern world have been generously imputed to protestantism by some very authoritative voices.

Protestants will object in their turn—and they will be right in view of certain facts—that catholicism is *also* and in consequence a type of government and discipline which suppresses personal liberty; which leads to domination; which places a human creature on the throne of Christ who is the sole head of His church (Pius XII demanded "absolute filial attachment to him who is the head and the foundation of the church, to the living Christ on earth, to the supreme Roman pontiff . . .":[1] the pope is thus described as the head and the foundation of the church; more; he is called "*the living Christ on earth*"); that catholicism is a type of faith which distorts the dogma of redemption, perverts religious faith into intellectualism and tolerates, indeed, sometimes

[1] Pius XII: "Wireless message on the occasion of the 4th centenary of the death of Ignatius Loyola". *Documentation catholique*, 19th August 1956, c. 1032.

promotes, forms of worship where credulity and idolatry take the place of true faith, etc. Why go on? Protestant polemics neglect no opportunity of replying to catholic polemics, which retaliate in full measure.

Once again, on both sides, these complaints are well founded. Not that protestantism is everywhere and always what it is criticized as being at times. No more is catholicism. But a sufficient number of facts, facing a fair-minded and impartial observation, justify these criticisms on either side. Charity has nothing to do with the present analysis; truth requires that both protestantism and catholicism should recognize themselves for what they are. Ecumenical peace has nothing to gain from a hasty dressing of the wounds of God's people.

Protestants will doubtless find it easier, at least outwardly, to recognize the wretchedness of the church, while at the same time praising God that He should permit His work to be carried on—in spite of the weakness of man's faith—through the manifestation of the power of His word in Jesus Christ. Catholics will say basically the same thing in other words; recognizing that the church is a church of sinners, they will affirm "that one cannot dissociate the concrete church from the reality of sin, that the church in this world is necessarily a society of sinners".[1] "The church in its concrete but adequate sense is both holy and full of sins, both faultless and fallible, both perfect and subject to multiple historical imperfections. That which, within its bosom, springs from the Christ, is holy and stainless. That which, within its life, springs from human liberty, is liable to defect."[2] Worthiness of the Christ and of His church, the church which He edifies; unworthiness of Christians and of the church which they shape and misshape. Power of the eternal Christ manifest in the weakness of historical men. . . .

It will thus be agreed that the appearance of the two spiritualities, catholic and protestant, is in reality more

[1] J. Galot, S.J., "Marie et l'Eglise", *Nouvelle Revue Théologique*, 1959, No. 2, p. 122. Consult for the same sense: G. Dejaifve, S.J., "L'Eglise catholique peut-elle entrer dans la repentance oecuménique?" *Nouvelle Revue Théologique*, 1962, No. 3, pp. 225–39.

[2] Y. Congar, *Vraie et fausse réforme dans l'Eglise*, 1950, p. 128.

complex and ambiguous, and, unfortunately, often enough rather remote from those basic principles on which we have tried to throw light. The reflections put forward above were not meant to be an exhaustive account of the characteristics which these two spiritualities, protestant and catholic, have developed in the course of their history and in the concrete forms, sociologically defined, which they have in reality assumed. The derivative and aberrant forms of catholicism and protestantism are not, however, without a certain interest for our instruction.

To note that they exist is sufficient for our purpose; for they show and they impose on our minds the irresistible conclusion that each of the two heritages, connected with the names of Abraham and Moses, has its own characteristic logic, its natural inclination; that a sort of fatality tempts each of them to exceed the limits within which it remains its own true self, so that both tend to degenerate, by the effect of this gravity, into a caricature of themselves. Gradually and imperceptibly each slides, from the authentic spirituality which it is, into forms of that spirituality which we must have the courage to denounce as adulterated. Neither catholicism nor protestantism has always been able or willing to disown and dissociate itself from such by-products. More often, the preoccupation with catholics has been to condemn protestantism, and with protestants to condemn catholicism. Both have been motivated by the secret fear of giving hostages to their opponents if they rectified an internal situation in the light of the opponents' critique; they have not wished to appear to admit the force of criticism by correcting excesses in conformity to objections made. For example, catholics do not find it easy to recommend the current reading of the Bible, just as protestants are reluctant to recommend a better balanced doctrine of the ministry, seeing that catholicism has made of the priesthood the cornerstone of its ecclesiology.

As a result of the interaction of the gravities natural to these two systems and the unhealthy fear which they have evinced, the two spiritualities have not yielded, within the framework of historic catholicism and protestantism, the fruits which they should naturally have produced. The fact is that they have developed unilaterally. They have not benefited by kindly and creative confrontations. They have yielded gradually to the one-sided emphasis inherent in their system and to the temptation of lapsing in the direction to which one is inclined. Lack of balance has been the result of their division. It will disappear only if believers agree not to hide from themselves the fact that Holy Scripture propounds and justifies two types of faith, two spiritualities, two spiritual and theological universes.

The first difficulty will assuredly be for each of the two sides to emerge successfully from its doctrinal and emotional ghetto in order to explore, with the sympathy indispensable for any deep understanding, the spiritual and theological landscape which had previously remained alien to it. To be sure, such an exploration, such an uprooting, will be easier if both sides attempt to go back to basic principles and propositions, to essential intentions. Protestantism must be judged, not by what it is, but by what it intends and claims to be. Similarly with regard to catholicism. It is not merely a lack of charity, but also a voluntary self-deception, to linger over the aberrations, the by-products, the malformations. It is right to judge the tree by its fruits, but not by its rotten fruit. Unfortunately we are so made that, in order to forget the rotten fruit in our own garden, we like to count the rotten fruit in our neighbour's garden!

Perhaps the attempt made in the preceding pages will result in facilitating the understanding of each of the two confessions for those who do not belong to it. Perhaps the reader will find in our arguments the opportunity of discovering the basic certitude lying behind and inspiring the successive stages of their development. Perhaps he will discern the coherence which, based on the wealth of implications inherent in the initial revelation, presides over the elaboration of the various elements, and imparts to them their authentic significance. Perhaps protestants will be moved not to judge catholicism on the basis of their own protestant premises, and catholics likewise not to judge protestantism in the light of their own catholic principles. For it is naturally thus that people proceed, and they will not act differently so long as they remain fettered to a unilateral reading of Holy Scripture. For if we think that scripture shields with its authority only that spirituality on the axis of which we ourselves are revolving, we cannot, from this partial standpoint, do otherwise than condemn as erroneous whatever cannot be reduced to it. If, on the other hand, Biblical revelation offers us a more complex spirituality, one in its source and object but dual in its human culmination, then it becomes necessary to free ourselves from the unilateral perspectives imposed on our judgments by confessional habits of thought, and to adopt a new point of view. What is this to be? In other words, how shall we conceive the possibility of conserving in harmony with each other the two spiritual heritages of Abraham and Moses? How shall we arrange their coexistence?

The difficulty of the question thus raised is evident. We can do no more than introduce a train of thought in this connection, so complex are the theoretical and practical, theological and ecclesiastical, problems involved.

Let it be understood from the outset that we cannot conceive the coexistence of the two spiritualities, Abrahamic and Mosaic, in the forms which these have assumed in historic protestantism and historic catholicism. Coexistence, to be peaceful, must be critical; not polemical but critical, positively and creatively critical. In scripture, the unity of the two spiritualities is attained at a level of depth which can be secured only on the express condition of getting rid of the superstructures wrongly added by circumstances of all sorts to the constitutive data of these two types of revelation. Both protestantism and catholicism must be "criticized" so as to eliminate these superstructures which stifle in them the living and authentic forces of the original revelation, and which make them "religions" in the worldly, political, social, psychological, ideological sense of the term; religions in fact which are secularized. Furthermore, the two confessions must be criticized so as to eliminate from them those deviations which they have suffered in consequence of the fact that they have developed in a spirit of competition, often of hostility, each believing itself obliged to repudiate systematically whatever characterized the other.

There can be no doubt about the welcome which will greet this work of "criticism" or auto-criticism, which nevertheless is so necessary and legitimate. Traditionally held positions will be bitterly defended. Men in general, and in this matter Christians are men like others, find great difficulty in freeing themselves from occasional consequences in order to adhere to basic principles; they cling to the tradition which has nurtured them, and, without caring whether or not it may have deviated from the original inspiration which was its source, they believe that they are defending the latter in cleaving obstinately to the former. Resistance will spring not only from the bench of doctors; the lay congregations will panic at the idea that the type of spirituality which is familiar to them might not be the sole legitimate one, at the idea that its very isolation may perhaps have deeply injured it. Further, we must not imagine that loyalty to tradition and the spirit of conservatism have altogether spared protestants. Although they have no firm doctrine of tradition, no commission of the Holy Office appointed to watch over the preservation of the faith, they are none the less firmly attached to "the inheritance of their fathers".

Again, the static attitude does not always lie in the direction one might suppose. The future may hold some surprises in store for those who claim, with somewhat facile assertion, as their motto: *ecclesia reformata semper reformanda*. In recent years, at the very heart of catholicism, there has emerged a Biblical movement which if continued may one day overtake protestantism. Who would have believed this possible in the days when Rome fulminated anathemas against the societies for the propagation of the Bible?

It is no impoverishment that will be produced by critical examination—an examination to which we must proceed if we wish to re-establish at least the conditions of coexistence between a protestant spirituality which has become once more authentically Abrahamic and a catholic spirituality which has returned to its Mosaic sources. The two spiritualities, restored to their fundamental inspiration, will rediscover their vitality through the fertilizing influence which each will exercise upon the other.

We must in fact realize the wrong that they have inflicted on each other by their mutual isolation. In the evolution of the confessional traditions the inheritances of Abraham and Moses have been weakened and, as it were, subjected to a process of anaemia. The essential nature of the Abrahamic type of piety, consisting of liberty and spontaneity, has been cooled, diminished in energy, hardened. The prophet, in order to be truly himself, must be freed from all institutional responsibility. He must be able to put forward his eschatological vision without having to worry about historical culminations. It is only at this price that he will be able to illuminate and correct the prudential judgment, and prevent it from becoming utilitarian or machiavellian. For, equally, the essential nature of the Mosaic piety, consisting of the concern for tradition, of loving maternal care, has been deadened, emptied, made sclerotic, because it has not received from the Abrahamic stream of inspiration the oxygen that would have released its efficacy. The concern for efficiency, for earthly embodiment, is a threat to the exercise of every institutional ministry. All too easily the priest becomes entangled in clericalism. It is the office and duty of the prophet to warn him of the law of entropy which threatens progressively to lower the level of his spirituality.

In other words again, the spirituality stemming from Abraham develops its promises if the Mosaic spirituality provides it with a sphere in which to act, a material to animate and quicken. On its side, the spirituality stemming from Moses develops its promises if the Abrahamic spirituality acts upon it as salt and leaven. The word is event; it must emit its resonance, otherwise nothing happens. Yet this word must not get lost in the limitless horizons it unfolds; there must be grouped around him who utters it those who are to hear it; it must in some way be conveyed to their understanding; it must be explained and applied to them. The event demands the genesis of the institution and the event alone justifies the institution, just as the institution presupposes the event and the institution alone can give the event earthly concrete expression. The word without the church is a celestial abstraction; the church without the word is a society of this world.

Thus the Abrahamic spirituality which is centred in the event of the word, and the Mosaic spirituality which is centred in the institution of the church and the sacraments, find their true unity in the service which they render each other. The solidarity which binds them organically together renders them indispensable to each other. Each finds in the other its full justification.

To be authentically in line with its Abrahamic source, protestantism must avoid the danger of self-confinement to its own traditions, of finding in its own mentality its end and aim. An Abrahamic protestantism will seek to escape the sclerosis involved in auto-justification. Likewise, catholicism, to be authentically in line with its Mosaic source, will avoid self-confinement and renounce the vain attempt to find in its own mentality its end and aim; for catholicism also, that is the condition of escaping the sclerosis of auto-justification.

It will be said: to what do these words amount, to what reality do they correspond? What, then, is a protestantism which aspires to be integrated with catholicism and a catholicism which wills to be one with protestantism? What is the meaning of this dreamlike theology? Where does this frenzied ecclesiology lead us?

I am not a prophet and I have no ready answer to these questions. I will content myself with adding two observations to the preceding analyses.

The situation in which Western Christianity is involved as a result of four centuries of division, following upon five centuries during which the west was cut off from the Eastern Orthodox tradition, now imposes on us a very unfortunate alternative when we think about relations between the two great western confessions; the alternative of either polemics or eclecticism. The reformers thought in terms of the church which they intended to reform; they "reacted against", they were opponents. The theologians who answered them thought in terms of the reformation which they wished to refute and abolish; they, too, "reacted against" and were opponents. Thus polemics seemed to become an inevitable function of theology.

In their endeavour to escape this accursed cycle Christians have been tempted by the alternative of eclecticism. On the pretext of charity, they close their eyes; they make artificial borrowings; they try to patch up frail and slender reconciliations. Thus they give pledges of their good will, but nothing is in reality changed. No problem will be solved by seasoning protestantism with a sprinkle of catholicism, or catholicism with a sprinkle of protestantism. The eclectic attitude is no better than the polemic attitude.

A solution of the situation is conceivable, however. If protestantism were to become authentically Abrahamic and catholicism authentically Mosaic, they would then be themselves in the best sense of the term and then precisely would be freed from the fatal necessity of opposing each other. Each would be able to affirm the other without disowning its own tradition.

They would thus become complementary and integrated with each other in a church which would no longer be what the catholic and protestant churches are today. Must we say—in a church which would be neither protestant nor catholic? Or must we say—in a church which would be both protestant and catholic? Both formulae are correct; for the first expresses what it would be necessary to change in the two churches as at present constituted, and the second suggests what it would be necessary to maintain in each of them. The new and twofold reformation necessary to render protestantism truly Abrahamic and catholicism truly Mosaic would imply both continuity and change for each of them.

Integrally bound together and complementary to one another; such are the spirituality derived from Abraham—the source and justification of protestantism, and the spirituality springing from Moses—the source and justification of catholicism, while at the same time these two spiritualities constitute the critical principle of the two confessions. Each must fertilize the other and, in so doing, balance it.

It is evident that, in present circumstances, it is impossible to imagine by what means could be taken in hand a reformation which would remove from contemporary catholicism and protestantism erroneous accretions which cause them to deviate from their true vocation and prevent them from being, at the heart of one and the same church, the two complementary spiritualities whose dialogue would promote the church's health and vitality. It is not even possible to imagine the emergence of such a constructive coexistence. In speaking of it, we seem to be speaking the language of visionary fanatics. Every Christian, in his confessional affiliation, comes up against the categories of thought imposed on him by his background of spiritual culture, even when the ardour and generosity of his faith awakens in him the desire to overcome these limitations.

We are not asked to eat today tomorrow's bread, but to pray that our daily bread may be granted us. The task for today, the task to which the pages now drawing to a close have been dedicated, is first of all and quite simply to recognize that fidelity to scripture, demanded by protestantism and catholicism alike, instead of being the occasion and the food for mutual antagonism, should rather be the occasion for a profound revision of judgment which each makes upon itself and upon the other. In trying to rediscover the principle lying behind each of the two spiritualities flowing from scripture, we shall discover at the same time their basic justification and the need to purify them from the distortions which have made impossible and unthinkable their coexistence at the heart of one and the same church.

Taking a human view, this is a task so difficult and so contrary to the natural dispositions of man that it would seem to belong to the domain of dreams and utopia. None of us will be able to see it completed. Happily, however, the views of the Lord for His people are to be measured, not by our weakness, but by His strength. The Spirit blows where it wills and when it wills. It may even inspire in theologians the desire to construct a dogmatic system which would take full account of the dual structure of Biblical spirituality.

Although Christian spirituality has two main sources, it offers us in the course of history manifold and varied forms. Hence the reader may have been surprised that we appear to reduce these forms to the sole dimensions of catholicism and protestantism. He will wonder in particular why no account has been taken of Eastern Orthodoxy or of Anglicanism.

This double silence does not imply either forgetfulness or ostracism. The theoretical and practical importance of these two great confessions can escape no one's attention.

If the author has discussed only catholicism and protestantism it was in order to facilitate the exposition and the understanding of the problem broached. Catholicism and protestantism enable us to see more clearly the features of those two types of inspiration which sustain Christian spirituality, for they have permitted the latter to develop up to the point where the lack of balance created by their mutual isolation has imparted to their respective characteristics an aspect of caricature. Hence we can the more easily see also what is specific and proper to each of them, and to what disadvantages we become exposed when the living solidarity which should bind them together is broken.

Some readers may be inclined to suggest that Eastern Orthodoxy and Anglicanism are well calculated to meet the wishes and aspirations which terminate our study. For do they not offer the example of spiritualities which have remained faithful to the double inspiration of the Abrahamic and the Mosaic faith?

This question deserves a separate discussion. But we must not exclude the possibility that Eastern Orthodoxy and Anglicanism have been successful in achieving a compromise rather than a synthesis. The critic may ask himself whether each of these two inspirations has really preserved, in the spirituality of the two churches in question, its entire density and dynamism. It is a question to be considered.

In any case, faithfulness to the two sources of Christian spirituality must lead us to set aside any scheme of co-existence which conceals the threat of their neutralizing, rather than stimulating, each other. It is through a tension sustained by a dialogue in which each questions the other and allows itself to be questioned, that—so it would seem—might be most usefully realized the unity of the Abrahamic and Mosaic spiritualities at the heart of the one church.

Index

ABRAHAM, Abrahamic spirituality, 17, 23–35, 38–42, 44, 50, 51, 54, 57, 61–71, 74, 75, 77–82, 91, 93, 94, 96, 103, 105, 109, 111–115, 117
Anglicanism, 117

BAPTISM, xi, 59
Bible, scripture, xi, xii, 13, 15–22, 42, 43, 56, 62, 67, 74, 78, 79, 82, 83, 86–89, 95, 107, 109–112, 116
Burning bush, 35–37, 45, 47, 48, 52, 53, 67, 69, 71–73, 99

CALVIN, 79, 80
Catholicism, *passim*
Colossians, Letter to, 20, 55
Corinthians, Letters to, 20, 55, 56
Cross, the, 24, 52, 53, 57

EASTERN ORTHODOX CHURCH, 75–77, 79, 114, 117
Ecclesia, 54, 56
Ephesians, Letter to, 20, 55, 97
Eschatology, 33, 50–52, 66, 68, 76, 77, 90, 93, 113
Eucharist, Lord's Supper, 56, 59, 76, 99, 100

FAITH, 16, 22, 23, 26, 29, 30–34, 37, 41, 43, 44, 46, 48–50, 53, 55–57, 60–63, 65–74, 87–96, 99, 102, 105, 107, 108, 110, 112, 116
Fideism, 88, 89
Filioque clause, 76
Fourth Gospel, 57–60

GALATIANS, Letter to, 20, 23, 33, 55, 56
Grace, 22, 30, 33, 34, 51, 63, 64, 66, 84, 85, 91–95, 101, 104

HEBREWS, Letter to, 29, 43, 72, 102
History, xi, 13, 21, 25, 28, 38, 44–46, 48, 50, 57, 58, 61, 68, 69, 76, 82, 89, 91, 93–95, 108, 109, 111, 113, 116
Holy Spirit, vii, 52, 55, 58, 76, 77, 83, 91, 92, 116

INCARNATION, ix, 37, 73, 77, 93–95, 97, 98, 102

JAMES, 25
Jesus Christ, ix, 17, 18, 22, 24, 30, 48–60, 64, 75–77, 79, 80, 82, 87, 95–99, 103, 104, 107, 108, 116
Johannine theology, 57–60
Judaism, Jews, 23, 26, 27, 37, 43, 50, 58, 78
Justification by faith, 20, 23, 55, 85

LAITY, vii, 98, 112
Law, Mosaic, 24, 38, 43, 46, 55, 56, 80
Logos, 57, 58, 60, 99
Luther, ix, 21–23, 78–81, 83, 90

MEDIATOR, 39, 40, 45, 67, 98, 103

INDEX

Moses, Mosaic spirituality, 24–
26, 31, 32, 34–43, 45–47, 50–
54, 56, 58–61, 67–75, 77–82,
92–96, 98, 102–105, 109,
111–115, 117
Mysticism, 73, 103–105

NAME OF GOD, 39, 40, 60
Nature and grace, 93, 97

PAUL, 23–25, 27, 28, 43, 54–57,
62, 64, 75, 78, 88, 90, 96, 97
Peter, 18, 23–25, 54, 75
Pope, vii, 23, 78, 107
Prayer, 91, 103
Priest, priesthood, 43, 44, 46,
47, 76, 77, 97–99, 103, 109,
113
Prophet, prophecy, 35, 39, 43,
44, 48, 55, 61, 80, 92, 113,
114
Protestantism, *passim*

REFORMATION, 21, 24, 78–81,
91, 114, 115
Revelation, xi, xii, 16, 29–31,
35, 37, 38, 41, 43, 45, 58, 59,
67, 70, 74, 96, 98, 111
Romans, Letter to, 20, 23, 33,
55, 56

SACRAMENTS, 46, 87, 97, 99, 101,
114
Sacrifice, 29, 30, 33, 46, 47,
52, 53, 56, 62
Sinai, Mount, 35–39, 45, 52,
60, 69, 71–73

VATICAN COUNCIL, vii
Virgin Mary, 87, 94, 95, 103

WORD OF GOD, 17, 18, 20, 26,
31–33, 39, 40, 44, 48, 50,
53, 55, 57, 60–62, 64–66,
71, 82–92, 95–99, 101, 102,
108, 113, 114

DATE DUE

JAN 20 1966			
NOV 26 1968			
OCT 28 1971			
GAYLORD			PRINTED IN U.S.A.